The Hum

The Hum

CALL AND RESPONSE
IN AFRICAN AMERICAN PREACHING

Evans E. Crawford
WITH THOMAS H. TROEGER

ABINGDON PRESS
NASHVILLE

THE HUM: CALL AND RESPONSE IN AFRICAN AMERICAN PREACHING

Copyright © 1995 by Abingdon Press

This book is printed on acid-free, recycled paper.

Library of Congress Cataloging-in-Publication Data

Crawford, Evans E.
  The hum : call and response in African American preaching / Evans
E. Crawford with Thomas H. Troeger.
    p.   cm.
  Includes bibliographical references.
  ISBN 0-687-18020-1 (pbk. : alk. paper)
    1. Afro-American preaching. 2. Afro-Americans—Religion.
I. Troeger, Thomas H., 1945–   . II. Title.
BV4208.U6C72   1995
251'.0089'96073—dc20   94-40262
                                                                    CIP

Scripture quotations, except for brief paraphrases, are from the New Revised Standard Version Bible, Copyright 1989 by the Division of Christian Education of the National Council of the Churches of Christ in the USA. Used by permission.

98 99 00 01 02 03 04 — 10 9 8 7 6 5 4

MANUFACTURED IN THE UNITED STATES OF AMERICA

Acknowledgments

*D*uring a career of thirty-five years of university chaplaincy, I have been blessed with numerous opportunities to preach, teach, and learn with and from the best. I came to the field of homiletics and preaching primarily by association. My academic major in theological studies centered in the discipline of social ethics although most of my seminary teaching has been in homiletics and preaching. University privileges afforded me numerous contacts with some of the most dedicated and articulate preachers, speakers, and singers whose gifts have established a cherished tradition of spirituality at Howard University's Andrew Rankin Memorial Chapel. It is from that background that I humbly attempt to share some insights on proclaiming the Good News.

I am grateful to many who laid foundations for my pathways to ministry and service. I thank God for Rosie Crawford, my grandmother, who guided me safely over many stony roads after my mother died when I was age three. Born and reared soon after Emancipation and denied the opportunity to attend school and learn to read, she exercised and embodied a loving and caring chastisement—the kind she claimed hurt her more than it did me—that made sure regular schooling was central in my growing years. Because of the way she channeled God's amazing grace to me, her family, and many others, I dedicate the book to her and give honor to God.

My part in this volume grows out of a fellowship of imaginative endeavors in teaching preaching with my colleague, Tom Troeger. Since my early lectures in ethnic awareness at the Colgate Rochester Bexley Hall in Rochester, New York, he and I have shared in the excitement and high privileges of preaching and teaching. His musical and poetic abilities have been a source of sharing that has enhanced my teaching and research, and I am grateful for the fellowship in study and service.

The core ideas and effort of my part of the volume, although elaborated and expanded here, were presented at the twenty-third Edwin E. Voight Lectures in Preaching in January 1989 at McKendree College in Lebanon, Illinois. I am grateful to the host committee and those who attended for their kindness and critical participation.

Sharing in all my efforts at ministering in higher education all of these years has been my wife, Elizabeth P. Crawford, who has been a source of information and inspiration in all aspects of the writing and research related to my preaching and teaching. I am grateful to her for being so generous with her God-given gifts and for her spirit of encouragement and support.

Contents

Foreword

This book invites you to enjoy a good conversation with a wise, experienced preacher. It is not so much an argument for a particular way of proclaiming God's word as it is a witness to the rich traditions of African American preaching. Evans Crawford is convinced that the value of those traditions is not limited to the group that gave them birth. He draws upon the particular character of his own background to illumine aspects of preaching that are important to every worshiping community: the interrelationship of the Holy Spirit, the preacher, and the congregation and the nature of the transaction that takes place among them as the word of God is proclaimed.

Evans Crawford models through his writing style the oral-aural tradition from which he draws his homiletical knowledge. Just as an effective preacher may not move forward in a straight line but may spiral around a central point, helping us to see it from many perspectives, so too Evans Crawford keeps returning to certain themes that help us to see more and more deeply into the mysterious depths of preaching.

For example, Crawford begins by naming some of the

most common patterns of verbal response that are offered by African American congregations as they listen to a sermon. At first, it seems like a simple observation of a particular people's customs. But Crawford leads us beyond the surface phenomenon to consider the theological and spiritual dynamics that are represented by this pattern of interaction. Soon he is reflecting on how these forces represent human yearnings and motions of the Spirit that are moving through the hearts of all people who hunger for the word of God and who offer thankful responses, silent or aloud, when they are fed. Thus he is able to draw on the traditions of African American worship to illumine what they reveal about preaching in a variety of cultural settings.

Crawford also describes the practical uses of pause, silence, musical phrasing, and the poetics of rhythm and alliteration, and then moves on to consider their deeper spiritual and theological significance. The book, while alive with down-to-earth practical advice for preachers, is always more than merely a technical guide. Crawford uses his observations about method and technique to reconnect us with the authentic and enduring source of all homiletical renewal: the Spirit of God, who brings the Word alive in the hearts of both preacher and congregation as they work together to open themselves to the gospel.

These theological insights also arise out of Crawford's understanding of the situation of African Americans living in a society that has often treated them as "invisible." Drawing on African American poetry, fiction, and social analysis, he explores the nature of possessing a dual identity as both African *and* American. He considers how this has brought confusion and tension to his people, but how it has also been a source of creativity and insight for black preaching. And having demonstrated this for black Americans, Crawford then proceeds, with his usual graciousness to all people, to invite readers to consider the dual nature of their own identities as a source for understanding the shape and character of their preaching.

Throughout the book Crawford acknowledges his debt to Howard Thurman, the great black spiritual leader and theological thinker. If you do not yet know Thurman, you will know enough by the end of this book to want to make a deeper acquaintance with his original works. However, even while Crawford draws upon Thurman, James Weldon Johnson, Ralph Ellison, and other great black writers and thinkers, it is the depth and preacherly warmth of Crawford himself that gives these pages their special character.

Beneath the conversational tone is a lively mind, one that keeps seeing the implicit theological connections between the sonic characteristics of black preaching and central affirmations of faith. For example, Crawford develops a strong argument for understanding the call-and-response pattern of the congregation as a manifestation of the priesthood of all believers. Such behavior represents the lived enactment of this central Protestant doctrine: Everyone acts as a priest because everyone participates in receiving and celebrating the word of God.

As I kept conversing with Evans Crawford through these pages, I encountered something that I would hope for my own ministry and for the ministry of all preachers. Here is a man who is unmistakably clear about his own identity, who has a deep affection for his own tradition, and who draws upon all that is best in that tradition. Yet at the same time, this never becomes a way of retreating from the larger community of faith or the broader human family. Instead, it becomes a way of interpreting how preaching at its best engages the gifts and graces with which God has endowed all human beings. In other words, Crawford demonstrates through his conversation with us the spirit in which reconciliation and community building become possible. Claiming who he is becomes an occasion to invite others to understand their identity and values. By the end of the conversation with Crawford, we have a fuller understanding of how to preach the gospel in a pluralistic world: not by denying our central traditions but by using them to relate us to others whose traditions are different from our own.

This is a book, to use one of Crawford's favorite phrases, of "mystic harmonies," particularly the harmonies that sound in the service of worship when the Amen that is in the people's heart is called forth by the preacher. Then they are able with faith and joy to praise their creator, and through that act of praise they are empowered to love kindness, to do justice, and to walk humbly with their God.

T.H.T.

Starter and Sustainer Responses

Glory Hallelujah!

The point of loudest praise, highest joy, and praise to God.

Amen!

The truth is affirmed and the pitch is right for the people and Scripture passage.

That's all right!

There are Good News and gospel possibilities; the sermon is becoming persuasive.

Well?

You're hinting to the witness with a chantable refrain or "riff."

Help 'em Lord!

The search is on for connections, and we start out in need of prayer.

Chapter 1

HOMILETICAL MUSICALITY
FROM "HELP 'EM LORD"
TO "GLORY HALLELUJAH!"

*M*any of the preachers I have taught belong to traditions that encourage the congregation's oral response to sermons. Over the years I have devised a sermon evaluation form to match the character of the participant proclamation that is an essential part of their worship life. Instead of mere numbers or abstract standards of judgment, the form includes phrases drawn from the repertoire of congregational responses that are a part of the tradition of the preachers' communities:

1. Help 'em Lord!
2. Well?
3. That's all right!
4. Amen!
5. Glory Hallelujah!

The list is in no way exhaustive but only suggestive. The aim is to encourage a constructive response, with a bit of the playfulness and freedom of the black church heritage. I stress that students can add their own re-

sponse phrasing as long as it has some authentic resonance with the church.

Although rooted in the black church, the clarity and wisdom represented by these oral responses illumine a variety
of traditions. Even preachers not accustomed to spoken
response from the congregation find these phrases helpful
in understanding the silent encouragements of their listeners. All preachers, no matter what their background, would
like to move their listeners from praying "Help 'em Lord!" to
"Amen!" and "Glory Hallelujah!" That movement represents
not simply the preacher's desire to deliver a successful sermon, but the deeper yearning that draws preachers to their
calling in the first place: to awaken in others a sense of wonder and thanksgiving toward God.

This book is about the movement from "Help 'em Lord!"
to "Glory Hallelujah!" That transformation of spirit requires
far more than learning the tasks of exegesis and the development of a successful outline. As essential as these are,
their mastery is not the focus here. Instead, I want to look at
those qualities of preaching which encourage an authentic
response of "Glory Hallelujah!" from the human heart,
whether that ascription of praise is spoken aloud or uttered
through those sighs that lie too deep for words.

I aim to show how an important factor in awakening such
a response is the preacher's "homiletical musicality,"[1] the
way in which the preacher uses timing, pauses, inflection,
pace, and the other musical qualities of speech to engage
all that the listener is in the act of proclamation. This musicality represents something much deeper than method. It is
an expression of the holy God working through the
preacher and the community, and it requires a rigorous and
authentic spirituality on the part of both preacher and congregation.

The phrase "homiletical musicality" has certain consequences for the way I will be describing preaching. Instead
of the more common homiletical concepts—outline, devel-

opment, exposition, structure, and so forth—my language will reveal a musical understanding of the way sermons are *heard* and the oral response they awaken in listeners, who in turn are *heard* by the preacher and one another.

This emphasis on preaching as an oral event, as a sonic experience with musical qualities, is reflected in my belief that preaching is holiness in timing. Webster defines timing as "the regulation of the speed when something is performed, so as to produce the most effective results." Abraham Heschel's "holiness in time" in his book *Sabbath* sparked my appropriation of the idea.[2] I have added an "ing"—"timing" rather than mere "time"—to give it living color, to bring out the musical qualities I want to examine. This distinction between time and timing is preserved among musicians who say, "Anyone can beat time," but gifted conductors have a sense for the timing of phrases and rests, or for what I will call here the "pause."

The pause in the sermon is much more than a break in delivery that is used by skillful speakers. I see it as a metaphor of spiritual formation, as an acknowledgment by preachers that they must not cram the air so full of their words that they obscure the vast and silent mystery from which true speech arises. Sermon pause represents not only a rest from the sound of the preacher's voice, but an opening in the preacher's consciousness through which the musicality of the Spirit breathes so that the musicality of the sermon resonates with the living truth.

For me, the preacher who most perfectly embodied the sermon pause as a symbol of these deeper realities was Howard Thurman. Thurman always insisted that preaching cannot be taught. As you can imagine, it is a claim to which I as a teacher (possibly doubting my job security!) vigorously objected. Although my primary academic credentials were in social ethics, I still felt that his claim was too sweeping. I came to realize, however, that his doubt was not whether preaching could be taught at all. Instead, Thurman was skeptical that it could be taught in any purely systematic way that ignored basic and fundamental spirituality.

And yet Thurman, as a person of "creative encounter" whose central quest was for "common ground," could not be sufficiently accounted for by traditional views of "spiritual formation."[3] His views had mystical dimensions which, although they shared the contemplative postures of the tradition, also made room for confrontation. Thurman embodied what I would call a mystical militancy or a militant mysticism. This is reflected in his writing and in the very titles he gave his books. For example, he was able to hold in tension a more contemplative work such as *The Centering Moment* with *The Luminous Darkness,* in which he deals with issues of civil rights and some of its advocates and leaders.

Thurman's dialectic between contemplation and confrontation makes manifest in a larger context the pattern of pause and speech which marked the delivery of his sermons. In other words, the style of the preaching was a recapitulation of the larger spiritual dynamics that marked his whole life. And because Thurman's life and his speaking were so integrated, one being an expression of the other, his preaching conveyed with extraordinary power the sense of holiness in timing. The interweaving of contemplation and confrontation continued into the timing of his sermon, as he interwove pause and speech to give witness to how the holy One was working in his life.

How do we teach people to embody that kind of wholeness and integrity?

This interweaving is the implicit question which lay behind Thurman's skepticism about the teaching of preaching. For his understanding of preaching seemed to demand an approach whose substance and style were more properly anchored in spirituality than in the formal principles of homiletics as a pastoral art and an academic discipline.

Nowadays, we might use a word that is currently touted on our seminary campuses and in many of our churches. We might say that learning preaching involves "spiritual formation." Although this gets us closer to understanding the ultimate origins of homiletical musicality as embodied by Howard Thurman, the term is not quite accurate. Instead of the word "formation," I prefer the term "biformation."

Michael Kammen takes one of the psychosocial notions of Erik Erikson expounded in his book *Childhood and Society,* and demonstrates that it may be proper to talk of "an African-American Biformation," a shaping of identity, perspective, and expression that flows from being both African and American.[4] This process of "biformation" can be seen in the outstanding African American literary writer and critic, Ralph Ellison. He never sees himself as anything other than an "American writer," and this is because of, not in spite of, his grasp of the folk life, symbols, songs, and idioms of his people as a part of what it means to be American. W. E. B. Du Bois expresses this as a "felt twoness," partly African, partly American, which in response to a "dogged persistence" wins from their two "warring" tendencies a kind of consciousness that makes for "creative marginality."[5]

The biformative process and its consequent creative marginality would have been an inevitable part of Howard Thurman's spiritual development as a black man in America. That is why I prefer to call the process of preparation for preaching that I observed in Thurman and that I am exploring in this book "spiritual biformation." That term keeps before us the particular legacy of being black in America and its impact upon the homiletical musicality of African American preaching traditions.

All of this is perhaps another way of saying what Henry Mitchell meant in his early writing when he spoke of the black minister as bicultural. I am nuancing Mitchell's insight to include as well Erik Erikson's psychohistorical term "Biformity." The word reminds us that the developing musicality of black preaching through history involves more than simply the reformation of one dominant cultural stream. Instead, black preaching is involved in biformation;

that is to say, its dynamic character is marked by the complex dual nature of African American identity. Black preachers are not simply "formed," they are "biformed." And when there are fresh developments in black preaching they represent not just a new "reformation," but a new "biformation." I will often return to this concept in later chapters because it is crucial in understanding the cultural and social interrelationships that have shaped black preaching in the past and that continue to influence it in the present.

Biformation also has implications for preachers of other racial identities. By gaining clarity about the impact of cultural and social forces upon black preachers, they will discover a sharper awareness of how such forces are interfused with the shape and substance of their own spiritual development. They will come to understand the factors that give rise to the particular musicality of their own preaching, and how that musicality is a sonic manifestation of various social and cultural forces alive in them.

The concept of biformation also helps us to understand the creative marginality of preachers like Thurman, whose social location on the boundary of the dominant culture gave him creative perspectives that were not available to those standing in the center of power. The "ity" in marginality, like the "ntu" in Jahn's classic on African thought, is useful in giving an overview of African American preaching insights and development. Just as Janheinz Jahn in his analysis caught the various sensibilities of African society by noting what was common, and yet what was unique by noting the spread of "ntu" in Muntu, Bantu, hantu, and so on,[6] the same is possible in noting how reflection in black preaching extends Phillips Brooks' classic definition of preaching as "truth through personality." What is now being said about black preaching can be categorized in terms of truth through particularity, marginality, secularity, antiphonality, and ethno or theomusicality, and finally spirituality. To be sure these are a lot of "itys," but they may be helpful in discerning the state of reflections on black pulpits and preaching today.

These various "itys" give us the larger context for the development of an authentic homiletical musicality. They remind us that the sources influencing the sound from the pulpit and the sound of the congregation's response are tremendously various and complex. They provide for us the larger backdrop of the responses with which we opened:

1. Help 'em Lord!
2. Well?
3. That's all right!
4. Amen!
5. Glory Hallelujah!

We no longer hear these as *only* the response of the congregation to the preacher. They are in fact the prayers of the human heart for help, guidance, and praise, enacted in the environment of worship and proclamation, but representing the larger, continuous process of biformation in which the congregation and its members are involved throughout their days.

In tracing the complex sources as well as the practical arts of homiletical musicality, I find myself influenced by several other writers who have also written about the centrality of spirituality to black preaching.[7]

I am particularly indebted to Jon Spenser for the term "homiletical musicality," which he uses to analyze black preaching as a legacy of West African sensibilities that continues on in some black pulpits and pews today.[8]

While drawing upon these many different writers, my approach is purposely more experimental, a conscious drawing together of the elements of fine and folk art, cultural and spiritual processes, inspiration and carefully crafted rhetoric. I base this deliberate fusion of wide ranging and diverse materials on my reading of James Weldon Johnson's classic preface on black preaching.[9] I also base it on my observation that this manner of sermon creation and delivery is in fact the very process that the most effective preachers use in attaining a homiletical musicality that helps the entire congregation receive and celebrate the gospel. My goal is to bring to the level of conscious art insights of black preaching which I believe continue in the James Weldon Johnson–like struggles of thousands of preachers. I call their homiletical preparation and delivery "folk work," and I tend to see all contemporary writers on black preaching engaged in that same work as well.

This folk work was the strenuous spiritual effort that, as Howard Thurman realized, fed the effective preacher, and looking at the complexity of social and personal forces that it involves, I can understand why he doubted that preaching can be taught. But I am convinced that by drawing on people like him, like Ralph Ellison, James Weldon Johnson, and the scholars of black homiletics that I have mentioned, we can bring to consciousness an awareness of the many different streams that feed our folk work. We can locate those sources where we need to stand still and be silent so that we can receive the word from the deep wells of the Spirit and our own homiletical musicality can be fed.

These "Folk Work" assignments, however, are not for Blacks Only. African Americans, for example, may have to work on a delivery style that best suits their ability and aspirations, while a European American may wrestle with how to handle the cerebration of the head with the celebrative urges of the heart. An Asian American may work on how to blend the contemplative with the celebrative. They have implications for the variety of "biformations" that make up America, the Americas, and the world. My hope is that even while I draw from the particular riches of the black church, preachers of other cultures and traditions can find here a way of renewing their own homiletical musicality.

To learn in this way from the black church is to participate in the spiritual depths of racial reconciliation. For in doing so, those who are not black will find themselves beginning to understand what Du Bois called that "warring sense of twoness" in black culture. Du Bois understood the difficult situation of oppression which gave rise to this "warring sense of twoness," but he was also able to find what was positive in it.

In more recent times, three former Princeton students have called the twoness which African Americans embody "Diunity." They affirm how that twoness is not something necessarily divisive, but is something different. Diunity does not "make one out of many," but seeks instead to recognize that there can be "one yet many." Although the immediate concern behind the development of the term was to probe and plumb American race relations, it has proved useful in the analysis of human relations as a whole.[10]

The concept of diunity leads to a "diunital analysis" of the many ways in which the twoness of the African American experience shapes and nurtures the characteristic musicality of black preaching. Instead of imposing one unified understanding upon the wide range of black preaching practice, diunity suggests that we allow for the multiplicity of oral forms and responses that have grown out of the twoness of being African American.

As we explore more closely the essential elements of homiletical musicality, we will discover that there is in black preaching a "blessed diunity" as well as a "blessed trinity." For the twoness of the African American experience has brought spiritual and prophetic insights that have been essential to the survival of our people. Those insights have sounded in the musicality of our preaching. And in listening to that music we hear more than the particularities of our own oral traditions. We hear God's global call, which lifts all of us, no matter what our racial identity, above our state of social and internal contradictions to the level of communion and celebration. We leave behind our initial prayer of supplication—"Help 'em Lord!"—to join in the glad affirmation of praise: "Glory Hallelujah!"

Chapter 2

Sermon Pause:
Setting the Climate
for Participation

*O*ften we talk about the climate of a situation or organization. When conflict arises in an office or the boss is dictatorial, we say "the climate is bad." If diplomatic talks look productive, the news reports that "the climate is good for their talks."

"Climate" represents not simply the spoken word, the substance of the communication, but that more elusive yet vital reality of the context for our speech. It can also refer to the tone set by our speaking, as when we observe that a particular speaker "set a good climate for the entire conference."

The metaphor of "climate" reveals why the impact of preaching depends on so much more than the content of the preacher's message. And just as the weather that is reported by meteorologists is a function of complex variables, so too the climate of the sermon is a function of many factors.

Sermon Pause: A Silence Shared

We often ignore the climatic factor that is most obvious yet essential to all preaching: that our speaking is surrounded by silence and that it is in the "pause" of delivery that "sound" or "pitch" resounds or reverberates. It delights me to observe that Fred Craddock not only takes note of this fact but uses it as a keynote in his theology of preaching:

> *How one understands a word as an event in the world of sound depends to a great extent upon whether that word is experienced against a backdrop of silence or in a room of many words. We have all experienced sound that breaks the silence. . . . How noisy are our attempts to create silence. . . . But a break in the noise is not the silence which we are considering. . . . The silence being affirmed here is a primal reality.*[1]

Long ago I intuitively felt the importance of silence when I purchased a plaque in New Orleans containing the words "silence spoken here." That sign has been around the house for some years and is a constant reminder of a dimension of preaching that we often fail to utilize.

Perhaps no preacher in recent memory embodied silence better than Howard Thurman, the former Dean of Rankin Chapel at Howard University, Washington, D.C., and Marsh Chapel, Boston, Massachusetts. Thurman was considered a religious mystic whose meditations and writings inspired and still inspire a generation of spiritual questers. My course outline in preaching that deals with his life and thought is subtitled "the Mystic Harmonies of Howard Thurman." That phrase was suggested by the hymn "For the Beauty of the Earth" and the lines giving grateful praise for "the mystic harmony, linking sense to sound and sight."

Nobody made use of the pause like Howard Thurman. Students who have traveled hundreds of miles to hear him speak, have been known to call him great just for rising, standing at the pulpit or podium, rubbing his hands over his face, and looking skyward before uttering his first word. His pauses initially seemed to embody what speakers call "the dramatic pause." Yet the pause for which he is well known seems to go beyond the merely dramatic. The spells of silence that were a part of his speaking are related more to meditation, and are best called "meditative pauses" given what went before and after them.

The first time I heard Thurman pray, he took so long to speak that I raised my head and opened my eyes to see what he was doing. In time he began the prayer, but the lengthy pause left me wondering whether he needed all that time and whether, in fact, he was not being too dramatic. Later, when my wife testified that the prayer moment was one of the most meaningful she had ever experienced, I realized the extent to which my professional expectations and habits had caused me to miss what Thurman perhaps purposely wanted to share—his silence.

Of course, there was no way for me to know that at the moment, because I was hearing him for the first time. But it was also my wife's first time yet she was able to experience his shared silence.

Why couldn't I?

Was it a matter of readiness?

Somewhere along the line had I missed out on experiencing the role that silence plays in relationship to sound? Could it be that Thurman had caused me to face for the first time what listening really requires, and what it really means?

These are more than my personal questions. They represent an awareness all preachers need to develop: a sense of the vital role that pause and silence play in human speech and particularly in preaching.

If in the phrase "pause and silence" you hear echoes of that faithful apostolic pair, Paul and Silas, I confess that the oral resonance is deliberate on my part. I am trying to raise your awareness of and ear for the festive quality of speech that is enhanced by pause and silence.

Howard Thurman advanced my theology and spiritual formation through the use of pause and silence. The climate of silence he offered revealed my need to recognize its significance, and to accept it as something shared by the preacher with the entire congregation. I had majored so long in my concept of preaching as content that I had become deaf and blind to the importance of "climate." As I became more familiar with Thurman and his spiritual quest, I realized that in both his preaching and praying he sought not to pray for you but to create or establish a climate where he could pray along with you. If that is not participant proclamation, then I do not know what is. It is a true profile of a silence shared.

Such a silence is far more than a dramatic pause. Even when it can be so described, it represents a deeper dimension. Maybe it can be called a "devotional pause." Call it what you will, but it is something that starts before and goes beyond the dramatic pause. That is why I lift it up as a sermon pause and name it "a silence shared." It is one of the most crucial factors in shaping the climate of the entire preaching event. Here I join with Fred Craddock in locating my theology of preaching at the point of pause and silence.

In fact, I now consider the sermon pause the keynote and mark for seminarians who study and meditate in a chapel named after Thurman, which is located in a divinity school that is part of the university where his mystical marks of spiritual formation were devised and displayed. It is in his spirit that I find some of the elements of participant proclamation and a resounding of the people's amens.

Biformation: Where Pause and Silence Arise

The use of silence that I have been describing arises from the complex development of the black experience in America. Because I am not convinced that Thurman thought in terms of spiritual formation, I would use the term "biformation," which I introduced in chapter 1.[2] That word captures something of the reality that Thurman knew as a black preacher in America, and is the same quality of experience Du Bois articulated as a sense of "felt twoness" in trying to reconcile what is African and what is American for black folks:

> *It is a peculiar sensation, this double consciousness, this sense of always looking at one's self through the eyes of others, of measuring one's soul by the tape of the world that looks on with amused contempt and pity. One ever feels his twoness—an American, a Negro; two souls, two thoughts, two unreconciled strivings; two warring souls in one dark body, whose dogged strength alone keeps it from being torn asunder.*[3]

Ralph Ellison gave this sense of felt tension a central place in his writing. He symbolized it in classical form in his novel *Invisible Man* and his critical essays published in the book *Shadow and Act*. In essence he says that he is "invisible simply because people refuse to see me."

Moving back and forth between recognition and non-recognition results in an "either-or" experience—either I am or I am not. African Americans feel this tension in the day-to-day existential conflicts that extend into the social and economic conditions of their community.[4]

How they should handle these conflicts is a crucial issue which both Ellison and Thurman addressed. Ellison looked for what was transformational in human experience and used it as a norm by which to measure progress and development. Thurman talked in terms of "common ground" and felt that the metaphors of "growth" and "centering" best expressed his principal concerns, especially for what he called the human spirit. To grow and become centered was his way of shaping the biformation process for spiritual development. Understood in this light, biformation actually becomes a goal of preaching: That is to say, black preaching helps the community find a faithful and fruitful way of dealing with the realities of its felt twoness.

If we can think in terms of spiritual biformation, then it is possible to speak to the actualities not only of African Americans but also of Asian Americans, Hispanic Americans, and others. Insight from any of these groups can provide opportunities for enriching preaching and praise.

Certain ways of using pause and silence arise from spiritual biformation so that these qualities are not simply preaching techniques. They represent the strenuous forces of the preacher's soul claiming a people's heritage, in a society that has often tried to suppress their expression and communication. When pause and silence are fed by these experiential depths, the climate of the sermon is one that encourages people to participate because they sense through the delivery of the sermon the struggle, the pain, the joy, and the faith that belong to them as well as to the preacher.

Timing

In the context of what I call the sermon pause, the element of timing takes on a significance beyond mere speaking. I say "mere speaking" because, although speaking is a basic sign of orality, it must be conceived of in a way that is inclusive of silence. Perhaps the most vivid description of what I have in mind was written by Thomas Long in Don Wardlaw's *Preaching Biblically.* Thinking of the sermon "in architectural terms alone," he says,

> *obscures an important dimension of preaching, namely the temporal dimension. . . . A sermon takes place over time. . . . Since sermons have purposes broader and deeper than those of legal arguments, involve patterns of development which are often more intuitional than scholastically logical and more emotional than cognitional and involve not only the organization of content but also the organization of time, other images and metaphors are needed to illumine the task.*[5]

Because metaphors for preaching taken from the courtroom and architecture are too narrow, Long chooses one suggested by Frank Kermode: the metronomic rhythm of the clock as a basic image for structured time. It puts the emphasis on the interval between the "tick" and the "tock" and then attempts to characterize or name the nature of that interval. It is not a "dead silence" but a "live silence." It is a silence that organizes time, that invites us to think of time not as something passed but as something plotted. Such a silence is similar to what Gene Lowry talks about in *Doing Time in the Pulpit*.[6]

The metronomic "tick tock" is a useful metaphor for the type of participant proclamation that resounds Amens, because although Long underscores the extent to which it centers on *plot,* it can also be underscored for the extent to which it centers on *silence.* It is not a "dead silence," nor is it, in Thurman's words, "a noisy silence." It is an *anticipatory* silence, a silence that is heard as well as shared. This heard and shared silence reminds us that preaching is not something that is under the control of the preacher alone; it is a communal event that also involves hearers and others.

Conversation reveals how such anticipatory silence is a part of normal social intercourse. Consider, for example, two friends getting ready for a serious conversation over a cup of coffee. As one of them puts on the water and gets out the mugs, there will be times of silence, yet this silence will not seem dead. It will be charged with a sense of the importance of what they are about to share. The silence is anticipatory, and part of what makes it possible for them to share as close friends is their ability to coordinate their timing, their silence, and their speech.

Because preaching generally takes place in a large public space and involves communication among a body of people, the elements of pause and anticipatory silence that are common to the conversation of friends become magnified in their significance. The cycles of silence and speech come to express the preacher's *spontaneity* and *spirituality*. Pauses mark the pacing of the sermon and are a key factor affecting the "timing" of the sermon. Unfortunately, it is a factor that tends to be taken for granted or ignored altogether by some preachers.

Could this be the reason why orality has tended to be subordinated to what is written and scripted in preaching? Perhaps.

But whatever the cause, the important point is the significance of timing to the oral medium of preaching. Far more than being merely a dramatic technique, the sermon pause utilizes silence as a context for sound. Enlarging our capacity as preachers to employ silence in this way ought to be part of our spiritual formation or "biformation."

The Preacher's Spirituality: More Than the Mastery of Methods

To understand that pause and silence are an integral part of "speech" is also to gain a fuller comprehension of my earlier assertion, that preaching is "holiness in timing." Abraham Heschel has defined Sabbath as "holiness in time" and pointed out that while "we own space, we live in time."[7]

Identifying preaching as "holiness in timing" supports and enhances the distinction that Eugene Lowry has drawn between conceiving the sermon in spatial terms, as something to be constructed, and thinking of the sermon as a temporal reality, as a time continuity to be experienced.[8]

Defining preaching as holiness in timing also suggests the point Thurman often made that preaching cannot be taught. In saying this he was not joining those who, according to Craddock, were downgrading the importance of "how-tos" and methodology. Thurman was pointing to the significance of spirituality in preaching as well as in the whole task of ministry. Perhaps he was also trying to say how much more important *timing* was than *technique*. At the very least, Thurman was suggesting that an equal amount of time be devoted to timing as is devoted to technique in the teaching and practice of preaching.

If sermon pause as a keynote in preaching reinforces the importance of timing in preaching, it may also suggest a hermeneutic for preaching. More insight comes from the lines of the hymn "Dear Lord and Father of Mankind":

> *O sabbath rest by Galilee,*
> *O calm of hills above,*
> *where Jesus knelt to share with thee*
> *the silence of eternity,*
> *interpreted by love.*[9]

The poetry brings out more than the sense of a silence shared. It also suggests the hermeneutic of *interpreting by love.*

Such a hermeneutic is clearly more than mastering this or that oratorical device. Nevertheless, it has practical implications for the use of silence and timing, since these are the very elements of delivery through which the congregation will sense—or fail to sense—the love that shapes our proclamation of the gospel. If you doubt this, simply think back to sermons where the message may have been about compassion and understanding, but the incessant pace of the delivery never provided a sense of the space that love makes for other people. Then consider a sermon about the same realities in which the pause and silence, the tick and the tock were an oral-aural manifestation of the qualities being proclaimed. The preacher left space for your own response and engagement with the gospel that was spoken. In this case the delivery was congruent with the content. You experienced the preacher's act of communication as the hermeneutic of interpreting by love.

Although such a hermeneutic's final source is a heart moved by the love of God, there are principles for delivery which can make that love more apparent in the preacher's use of pause and silence. If these are employed simply as rote methods, then they will come across as wooden. The preacher's attempt to manipulate the listeners through methods. But if they are adopted as a way of allowing the most effective expression of the heart that has been moved by the love of God, then they will deepen and expand the sense of the hermeneutic of interpreting by love.

Augusta Baker and Ellen Greene have compiled a useful list of the practical principles for timing, pacing, and dramatic pause, and these are printed in a section of Bruce Salmon's *Storytelling in Preaching: A Guide to Theory and Practice.* As you read through them, I urge you to consider not only their immediate application, but also the symbolic and larger meanings they suggest in light of the hermeneutic of interpreting by love.

1. Pause before any change of idea or significant word.
2. Emphasize meaningful words.
3. Take imaginative passages slowly; take rapidly parts narrating action.
4. Change pace as the climax nears.
5. Employ conversation at a speed that is appropriate for the character speaking.
6. Note that the pause and the dropped voice can be more effective than the shout.[10]

If we expand this checklist to include the significance of pausing to convey spontaneity and spirituality, it includes as well the following suggestions:

1. Pause to heighten the participation so that in prayer you pray with the hearer, and in preaching you invite response.

2. Let your pauses do the talking and the timing.
3. Identify the "pausal moments" exegetically where the biblical narrator's perspective and theology break through.[11]
4. Let your pauses serve to punctuate silences in a way that keeps them organized.
5. Don't shout, share.

Once these elements of pause and silence engage the basic spirituality of the preacher, then sermon spontaneity cannot be far behind. The nature of the spontaneity we seek is akin more to what I call "homiletical musicality," in which pause, silence, and timing become expressive manifestations of both theology and preaching in a new key. The homiletical musicality is not merely an ornament added to the top of the substance of the sermon, but is rather the embodiment in sound and silence of the truth that is proclaimed.

Chapter 3

RESOUNDING THE PEOPLE'S AMEN

Adapting a Model from the Social Sciences

*E*ver since boyhood I have been part of a talk-back religious heritage that shares proclamation between the pulpit and the pew. The sermon belongs not only to the preacher, but also to the entire congregation, which joins in with their oral responses. In United Methodist churches, the talk-back has not been as notable in the congregations where I have preached as in many of the Pentecostal, Baptist, and independent black churches where I have spoken. Bruce Rosenberg, a student of medieval literature, has found some traces of the "talk-back" responses in the Appalachian churches in America and has drawn some conclusions about what he calls the American folk preacher.[1] There is a significant talk-back tradition in America, and although the nature of that response may be changing in some churches, it continues to be an essential element in assessing preaching.

This is what I now call "participant proclamation." I coined the phrase from a process called "participation observation," which I learned during my academic training in the discipline of ethics. The process of both participating and observing was conceived as a research method more adequate to the nature of work in the social sciences than in other objective sciences. Participant observation is a form of disciplined attentiveness in which the researcher acknowledges that she or he can gather certain kinds of information only by being present and therefore a part of the data. Such participant observers attempt to observe with as little disruption as possible so that another observer could replicate the encounter, if desired.

Assuming there is something experiential in gospel proclamation similar to sociological observation, I pair participation and proclamation as a means of understanding the aspects of prayer and praise that are a part of the congregation's oral response. Hence the term "participant proclamation."

Like all models drawn from one field and applied to another, the term has its limitations, but it does capture something of the participant observer role of listeners who respond to preachers. On one hand, the listeners observe, listening to and watching what is happening in the pulpit, and absorbing the verbal content of the sermon, and the vocal inflections and bodily gestures of the preacher. While on the other hand, they participate by adding their own verbal responses, which are sometimes coupled with a gesture of prayer or praise, such as a lifted hand.

However, unlike the participant observer role in the social sciences, the congregation's participation may sometimes arise from a desire to change the phenomenon. "Help 'em Lord!" is not a prayer of objective observation! The observers become active participants who encourage the Spirit and the preacher to bring forth the word of God more clearly. In this instance the sociological origins of the term "participant proclamation" become less significant than its theological ramifications.

Congregational Response as a Manifestation of the Priesthood of All Believers

Participant proclamation does more than describe what is actually occurring in churches where the congregation responds orally to the preacher. It strengthens and manifests one of the central principles of the Protestant heritages: "the priesthood of all believers." The congregation's responses and participation in shaping the act of proclamation makes it clear the preacher does not hold a hieratic monopoly on the word of God. The word is shared by the entire group.

It is significant to note that the literature on preaching in recent years has been emphasizing the congregation's investment in the sermon. Formal homiletics is providing support for a theology of participant proclamation. For example, the Reformation notion of the priesthood of all believers is again being stressed through the "inductive preaching" that Fred Craddock exhibits in theory and practice.[2]

The central affirmation of the sixteenth-century Reformers finds further practical application in George W. Swank's little volume, *Dialogic Style in Preaching*.[3] His discussion lifts to a higher level the particular liturgical manner of the more charismatic churches and folk-oriented churches. He accomplishes this in part by bringing a critical standard to the assessment of participant proclamation. He makes a distinction between monological and dialogical sermons, and shows that even in so-called talk-back churches, the preacher may deliver a unidirectional sermon that fails to engage the congregation in an authentic act of listener response. This reminds us that the presence of oral response does not *automatically* mean the congregation is participating in proclamation. "Amens" and "Glory Hallelujahs" can become as perfunctory as any other liturgical expression. But they can also represent the profoundest motions of the human heart, the Spirit's stirrings in the depths of the soul.

The People's Amen

Although I am helped by sociological and communications theory in understanding the phenomenon of participant proclamation, I believe its deepest origins are in what we can call "the people's amen," a phrase suggested by the closing stanza of the famous hymn, *Lobe den Herren,* "Praise to the Lord! the Almighty, the King of Creation!":

> *Praise to the Lord!*
> *O let all that is in me adore him!*
> *All that hath life and breath,*
> *come now with praises before him!*
> *Let the amen sound from his people again,*
> *gladly forever adore him!* [4]

I find in these lines a call to resonance, which is the source of the title to this chapter, "Resounding the People's Amen." We are made to resonate with an impulse to praise that sounds in the core of all things. We are created for response to God's eternal call, all of us, the world over: "All that hath life and breath, / come now with praises before him!" Congregations that practice participant proclamation are living out what the hymn-writer puts into words. They "Let the amen / sound from [God's] people again."

I have experienced how profound the desire is for people to claim the Amen that is deep in their hearts. Since my first pastorate in a Free Will Baptist church in Providence, Rhode Island, I have spoken of this claim as "Brother Ward's Amen." Brother Ward was a deacon in Pond Street Church. He was perhaps the only one in that congregation who was thoroughly accustomed to talking back to the preacher, and even his running response to the preacher had gradually fallen to one loud amen after the close of the sermon.

Other members of the congregation belonged more to the "feel-back" school of response. The silent attentiveness of their faces, rather than words, reflected their acute listening. There were persons of the "feel-back" disposition and manner who judged that Brother Ward's Amen came only after a sermon he particularly liked. Some even speculated that it was only a personal response, harmless but definitely on its way out. In actuality, it had more of a communal authenticity than was at first thought.

Another member, an in-service worker and maid, was also faithful, but full of "feel-back." She regularly attended and was always there to hear the sermon and Brother Ward's predictable response. One day she asked about brother Ward's several absences due to illness and hospitalization. When told about his illness, she asked me to convey best wishes and to tell him she missed his Amen.

I then realized that Brother Ward's Amen was more communal than personal. I wondered how many others felt the same way—even those who would not publicly sound an audible Amen. A spot survey revealed that most of those who "felt back" rather than "talked back" still identified with Ward's Amen. They acknowledged how it felt like an authentic Amen, an oral response which seemed to gather up the unspoken responses of their own hearts. Ward's Amen gave voice to the Amens that were silently sounding within them.

The Difference That Participant Proclamation Makes to the Preacher

More than perhaps Brother Ward knew, and certainly more than I realized, he participated in the proclamation at Pond Street. Those who "felt back" also participated, but it was the contribution of his spoken Amen which helped to focus and finally give substantive expression to that participation. Discovering the depths of response that were being articulated by that one loud Amen brought me to a new understanding of preaching and of the preparations I made for proclaiming the gospel. And I believe that there is a similar impact for other preachers. Once we realize how invested the congregation is in the sermon, then the misery of feeling alone in the pulpit ceases. We sense instead the abundance of God's mercy, which is present in the congregation, whom we now view as fellow participants in the act of proclamation. There is a spiritual shift in the preacher's soul so that the preacher does not preach *at* or *to*, but *with* the congregation. The direct benefit is that the communication barriers between pulpit and pew sharply decrease, while the corporate action of giving glory to God increases.

As in most cases, the benefits sharpen our awareness of our responsibilities. Being aware of participant proclamation, for example, presses upon us the need for a responsible pulpit to match a responsible pew, which includes both those congregation members who "talk back" and those who "feel back." This is especially true when there is evidence, as in the case of Brother Ward, that those who feel back identify with those who, even if their number is small, still talk back. We feel more responsible as preachers because we are aware that our function is not simply to deliver our message or version of the truth, but to awaken a sense of the word that is alive in the congregation, both in individual hearts and in the group as a whole.

However, the sharpened sense of responsibility does not belong to the preacher alone. Participant proclamation also calls for a responsible pew. This means faithful hearing from the congregation, what Leander Keck calls "priestly listening."[5] According to him, "priestly listening" is one way to consider the preacher's exegetical calling, but "priestly listening" ought to extend to the pew as well as the pulpit. He significantly notes in this connection, however, that the black church pew is an "exception" to the "loss of attentiveness to verbal communication, to oral discourse [that] has eroded the place of the sermon . . . for there it is often customary for the congregation to participate in the preaching with its 'amens' and 'right ons' [and] the same must be conceded to white 'pentecostal' churches as well."[6]

Practical Implications
and Strategies for Sermon Preparation

Such an understanding of the mutual responsibility of preacher and congregation leads to certain practical strategies for sermon preparation. As Don Wardlaw observes, "Active participation by the members begins with the sermon's conception rather than after its delivery."[7] William Thompson demonstrates one way this might work in practice. He outlines how lay people and clergy can share and concentrate on biblical readings from the lectionary for mutual exhortation.[8] If you try his approach, I urge that your resources for preparation include the *Social Themes of the Christian: A Social Commentary on the Lectionary,* to keep the sharing wholesome and inclusive.[9]

Don Wardlaw provides a sophisticated analysis of the theological and pastoral models that undergird such a method of group preparation for participant proclamation.[10] Wardlaw views the congregation as a corporate agent in the act of preaching who come to see themselves as partners in the process. In such a context, he says, the minister preaches as much *for* the congregation as *to* it. This will require, perhaps, not only a listener's guide to preaching but also a heralder's guide to listening. Benefits should include the ability to speak *with* God on behalf of the people and community.

Expanding the dimensions of participant proclamation into delivery does not mean that congregational members will be helping to prepare every sermon directly. But it does mean that they will always be key contributors to the creative process, from those who, on Sunday, will be feeling back, to those who will be talking back. The Amen of Brother Ward or Sister Jane—or whoever the bellwether is in your congregation—will be a part of you as you get ready for Sunday's participant proclamation.

And in the presence of those participants you will detect why you absolutely cannot afford any of the "rather flat, single dimensional orientations to preaching" that make sermons boring.[11] Your fellow participants in the proclamation will not allow it! They will keep reminding you of the inadequacy of understanding a sermon to be a "static, linear transaction, with the sermon to function as a message, the preacher as sender, and the congregations as passive recipients."[12] In other words, when people gather for preaching they seek sermons less for information than for inspiration and celebration. Such a concept of the sermon contains presumptions no longer valid or at least more suspect than before, especially when we think of preaching as participant proclamation.

And that concept is reinforced by theologians who have related Scripture more to an event and a happening than to an object with a database for sharing. This understanding of the Bible releases one to confront and actively engage the world, to join with the congregation in the corporate event of hearing and celebrating the word of God. No one wants to be left out of an event this exciting. Nor do they want to stand passively by. They want to join in, to participate along with everyone else. If they do not sound Brother Ward's Amen aloud at least it will be singing in their hearts.

In that Amen, spoken or silent, the congregation will experience a basic solidarity with one another, which represents the actualization of Jesus' promise "that where two or three are gathered in my name, there shall I be in the midst of them." In other words, participant proclamation leads to a rediscovery of the communal character of our knowledge of Christ as alive and present among us. Thus participant proclamation is more than the sum of practical strategies and methods we have been considering. It is the community's way of experiencing Christ as it gathers in his name to proclaim and celebrate the Good News he brings and the Good News he is.

The Many Resonances
of Participant Proclamation

The sense of Christ's presence that comes through participant proclamation awakens the church's ability to hear the deeper resonances of life which otherwise go ignored. I refer here to what James Weldon Johnson honored along with his brother when they composed the words and music of what is called the Negro or Black National Anthem, "Lift Ev'ry Voice and Sing." The poetry speaks of "lifting ev'ry voice to sing" liberty's harmonies and to let them not only rise but also "resound." That resonance has *height,* "high as the listening skies" and *depth,* "loud as the rolling sea"; it is another way of speaking, as the hymnist does in "Joy to the World," about a "sounding joy." Although the empirical philosopher might be skeptical of granting any objective existence to these resonances, they are precisely the realities the community of participant proclamation experiences in the act of preaching and responding. Some religious thinkers may be tempted to turn from considering such matters, deeming them the "soft" facts in a theology of preaching. But to ignore them is to ignore the hard empirical fact that it is this resonance of meaning and sacred presence which has given strength to millions of black persons to endure a brutal history. And this resonance continues to lift and empower worshipers in thousands of churches that practice participant proclamation.

I have drawn here on hymnic language because it requires rhapsodic expression to communicate "echoes of mercy" and "whispers of love."[13] I celebrate, however, that homileticians are beginning to take seriously the import of the sonic dimensions of preaching, as in Fred Craddock's recent attention to "silence, sounds and shout."[14]

Such theological attention keeps participant proclamation grounded in its ultimate source: the endlessly resonant

nature of reality from whom all our Amens and Glory Hallelujahs spring. To give voice to these expressions of praise
is to become a church that sounds with "a resonance for
life." This last phrase is deliberately designed to bring to
mind Albert Schweitzer's ethic known as a "reverence for
life."

Resonance for life.
Reverence for life.

Read them aloud. Hear in the air the kind of sonic connections that are an important element in participant proclamation. Of course, just because words sound similar does not
make them logically related. But in this case the similarity
of sound reinforces and heightens the ethical intent behind
my phrase "resonance of life." It is this fusion of sonic and
conceptual elements that is part of the joy of the sermons
that awaken participant proclamation. Preacher and congregation delight together in the beauty and power of the
sound as an expression, even a manifestation, of the content. So that, for example, if you could hear me as I speak
the words from this page, you might capture the delight I
take in the similarity of the two phrases:

Resonance for life.
Reverence for life.

That delight in my voice arises because the welcome echo
between the two phrases assuages a guilt I have had when
accused of abandoning the field of social ethics. I indicated
at the start of this chapter the process I used to marry
"proclamation" to "participant," which emerged from my
study of research in sociology. Although it is coincidental, I
am now able to speak not just of a reverence for life as an
ethicist, but also of a resonance with life as a homiletician.

The similarity of sound gives audible substance to a

yearning in my soul to make my life as a preacher congruent with my training as a professional ethicist. That in turn makes me more vitally engaged with what I say so that I too, can join more fully in the act of participant proclamation.

Although I can give a partial account of the personal reasons for my delight in the two phrases

resonance for life
reverence for life,

my joy in participant proclamation goes deeper to a mystical kind of understanding. It is best expressed in the hymn "For the Beauty of the Earth," especially the lines

For the joy of ear and eye,
  for the heart and mind's delight,
for the mystic harmony
  linking sense to sound and sight.[15]

These words bespeak my understanding of the realities of the soul that are engaged by participant proclamation. I find room in such preaching for the people's Amen and room to listen for the resonances that abound in God's world.

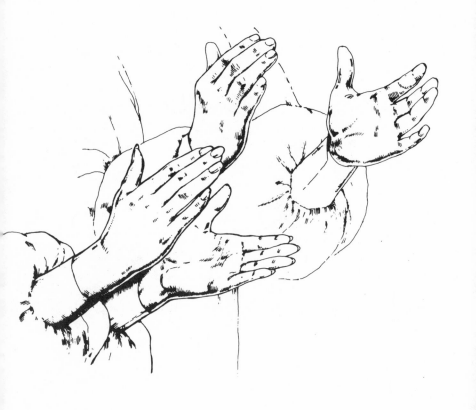

Chapter 4

HUM THOUGHT:
TALES, TUNES, AND TALK

For thirty years I taught where Howard Thurman first served as Dean of Rankin Chapel. If reading this book is the first time you have heard of him, it is understandable, for he, like many of his tradition and idiom, was an example of that phenomenon which Ralph Ellison named the "invisible man."[1]

When "being seen" is a matter of the beholder's eye, it often follows that there can be sights unseen and selves unseen. Likewise, if "being heard" is in the beholder's ear, there can be sounds unheard and sighs unheard. And the breakdown of sight and sound may reinforce each other so that the beholder's failure to see may result in a failure to hear, and the beholder's failure to hear may result in a failure to see. It is as if the senses confuse themselves in their mutual failure that results in sights unheard and sounds unseen.

Sights unheard and sounds unseen—I use this startling juxtaposition to sharpen our perception. It reveals, for instance, that you cannot hear for looking and you cannot see for hearing.

What I am describing here is the complexity that underlies our common English phrase the "beholder's eye," the realization that sight is not a simple matter of objectively registering the external world upon the retina. It involves instead a complex process of perception that is marked by the unique qualities of the one who is looking. And we can easily parallel the phrase "the beholder's eye" with "the beholder's ear," for in listening as in seeing we are involved in a complex process of perception.

The problem of the beholder's eye and the beholder's ear ought to be a central concern for all who preach and take seriously and responsibly the priesthood of all believers. For if we preach without considering how we will reach the beholder's eye and ear, then we ignore the peculiar gifts of perception that belong to the congregation, and in doing so we fail to honor what we claim about their priesthood in receiving, considering, and seeking to live the word of God.

The priestly task I speak about can be deepened by practicing what someone has called "perceptual creativity."[2] By listening carefully to all the sounds with the intent to tell and share them with the hearer, the beholder's ear is put on alert. Focused looking can do the same for the eye of the hearer as a beholder. When put in the context of gratitude to God, these two invite and evoke a reverence for the "joy of ear and eye" that shares with the other perceptual powers in "linking sense to sound and sight." This phrasing has the poetic and the rhythmic quality of James Weldon Johnson's *God's Trombones*. He caught it from the African American folk preacher who doesn't speak, say, of the mere "rising of the sun," but true to their tradition of beholding eyes, says instead: "I looked and saw the first thin pencil line of dawn, and watched God's ball of fire seek its noon meridian, continue its relentless journey to the twilight and then lay down to sleep beyond the western hills." Such description evokes a host of "amens" and the "glory hallelujahs" from priestly believers and priestly beholders.

Working Through the Sound to the Truth

This last paragraph, which initially appears as a digression, is actually an illustration of what I mean: the way sound engages my particular beholder's ear, and how I must work through the sound to come to the truth. Although your pattern is probably different from mine, most of us who preach are familiar with the problem. We want the sermon to sound right, to sound as right as "mystic harmonies linking sense to sight and sound."

I hear music when the issue of the beholder's eye and ear is put that way. If you ask me what kind of music or the name of the music, I must confess that I do not know. It may have a name, or maybe it seeks to have a name. All I can say is that there are moments when what breathes on and within me does not have a name I know. You can be sure however, that I am so awed I am going to discover its name.

Those of you reading this book and who seek the sound of the sermon that will engage the eyes and ears of your congregation are also seeking that name. It is not a search that goes in a straight line. Instead, it breaks out in ways that we do not quite expect, just as here in these paragraphs I have turned from essay to homily, one addressed to you my preaching colleagues.

In a sense this process of tracing the "mystic harmonies" as we move from analytical prose to homiletical reflection and rhapsody is the legacy of the apostle Paul at his best. Paul, right in the middle of his most forensic writing becomes lyrical and doxological, a moment we honor and share age after age, and Sunday after Sunday, by resounding it in our worship, praise, and especially our benedictions. "May the God of steadfastness and encouragement grant you to live in harmony with one another, in accordance with Christ Jesus, so that together you may with one voice glorify the God and Father of our Lord Jesus Christ." Amen (Rom. 15:5-6); "Now to him who by the power at work within us is able to accomplish abundantly far more than all we can ask or imagine, to him be glory in the church and in Christ Jesus to all generations, forever and ever. Amen" (Eph. 3:20-21).

Let these words resound in your ears as you read this. They remind us that it is not enough to talk about amens, affirmations, and acclamations. They must actually resound from us as part of our homiletical musicality, as an expression of the hum thought, which is not merely the ether of ideas floating in the mind but the sonic materialization of our insight and rapture.

My forebears knew about the irrepressible nature of this hum thought. Perhaps rebelling against attempts to limit prayers not found in the *Book of Common Prayer,* they simply sang, "Ev'ry time I feel the spirit, I will pray."

I say the same about preaching. It is, of course, easy to disparage such preaching by concentrating on the dangers that are implicit in such an approach; to point out how it can disengage the mind and leave an opening for bad spirits, for Satan to don the Spirit's clothing of spontaneity. But we need to remember here that a purely rational and controlled approach to preaching is just as susceptible to distortion and evil. Any approach can be turned from the purposes of God. To protect the integrity of hum thought requires the same theological integrity as any other homiletic: The Spirit that we feel inspires us both to pray and preach, is a tested Spirit, true to Pauline requirements, and wilderness-tested in a way to yield not to temptation.

I am taking time to write this on paper the same way as the preacher who is open to hum thought takes time to develop the sermon. The preacher does not merely want to say, speak, or articulate the Word. The preacher seeks to "sound" the Word so that people not only "hear" it but also "see" it.

At first this may appear as "nonsense" in order to get your attention. However, we can follow the individual sentences and can even see bits of meaning unfold, but the overall pattern is not yet clear. It may take a bit more time to engage your affection. But once it does, my faith, indeed, our faith, is that you will feel the holy Spirit and act in "responsible freedom." In other words, the development of the hum thought is a process that leads to moral consequences for the congregation by engaging the beholder's eye and ear in ways that awaken ethical capacities.

Moral Implications Expressed Through Sound

"Responsible freedom" is a "diunital"[3] phrase that Lynn Harold DeWolf, my systematic theology professor and Martin Luther King Jr.'s graduate study advisor, used as a title for one of his books on theological ethics.[4] It is a helpful term because it captures the generative work of God, which the preacher needs to express through the sermon. By "generative" I mean the way that God's words and actions generate possibilities for an ethical life. Just think of it: After the Egyptian exile, during the Exodus, Israel wrote an account or took special note of God's generative acts, words, and ways in order to understand their meaning for how Israel was to live. For example, one of the main tasks for Moses during the Exodus was discerning how to make Israelite freedom responsible. And that meant he had to address the murmurings and yearnings of the people in the wilderness. He was faced with the very questions we have been exploring: the beholder's eye and ear. How would Moses engage "the mystic harmonies linking sense to sight and sound"? The encouragement to a holy and ethical life would have to move through the complexities of perception that encounter every sounding of God's word.

Essentially, the Israelites were an "ear" people. The first word of the Shema was "hear," not "see." Of course, either sense could engage their perception, but the "eye" proved so fickle and was so easily seduced that among the first of the commandments was a prohibition against "graven images." And such images seemed to multiply everywhere in the wilderness. Graven cows were available in bronze or gold, and perhaps in any metal that existed. Before long it became clear that what was undertaken as an escape "to" freedom, all too quickly became an escape "from" freedom.

The remedy was not either-or, either freedom or responsibility. The remedy was in the act of holding both of them together at the same time, and in such a way that something could be experienced, embodied, and felt. Only then could freedom be regarded not as a formula but as something felt, something arising from the same depths of heart and soul where "the mystic harmonies linking sense to sight and sound" are found. There had to be a method of communicating "responsible freedom" that resonated with its source, in the heart that is open to God and that hears the Spirit moving through hum thought.

This is why I believe there must have been a quality of hum thought to Moses' preaching; a sense of the urgency and anger of God against idolatry must have materialized in the beholders' eyes and ears. Otherwise it would have failed to redirect their need for a tangible spirituality from idolatry to the service of God, their liberator. Moses' preaching must have empowered, not only by its content, but also by its character of hum thought, DeWolf's notion of "responsible freedom." Moses' way of sounding the word must have made credible the possibility of maintaining the tension between responsibility and independence, which is captured in the concept of "responsible freedom" and which illumines the truth that sets us free.

The Resonance of the Spirit
in the Hum Thought of the Preacher

This understanding of hum thought as an expression of the word of God that is congruent with all of its dimensions, including the ethical, helps us to claim with greater appreciation Phillips Brooks' famous definition of preaching as "truth through personality."[5] Truth comes through the particularity of the preacher's expressive mode, and what the congregation listens for in that particularity is the resonance of the spirit.

The church attempts through its liturgical and biblical structures to foster the resonance. For example, the compilers of the common lectionary have provided more reading from the Old Testament or Hebrew Bible so that we can hear God's resonance sounding through the particularity of the Scripture writers. The impact of these more extended readings is to remind us that the Bible, like life itself, is not a unison melody. It is more like a symphony that begins with a simple declared melody but develops a rich harmonic and thematic texture. When preachers draw upon this symphonic theological richness, their preaching begins "resonating life," and through that resonance we hear God calling us to respond.

"Resonating life" is a musical way of saying what the Gospel of John says about the purpose of Jesus' coming: that we might have life and have it more abundantly. Musically, I sense that to mean that we can have life more "antiphonally, polyphonically, and even symphonically." The "musical" richness of life in Christ is manifest in a sermon where hum thought awakens the hum thought of the listeners.

Call and Response
as an Expression of Life in Christ

A striking example of the musical richness of life in Christ is the antiphonal response of the listeners to the preacher in congregations that practice participant proclamation. I know it best as "call and response," which is a responsive chord created in the congregation and sounded back to the preacher and the rest of the congregation. Currently the response is not only a matter of talk-back—using a variety of expressions such

THE HUM

as "Well?" and "Stay right there"—but also a matter of feel-
back, manifested in gestures and body language.

Wyatt T. Walker, a noted pastor and preacher, tells of a
revivalist preacher who established a pattern of call and
response using the parable of the prodigal son. Under the
title "The Wonderful Father," he set the scene of a returning
son and a waiting father at the edge of the porch in a chair.
A week passed, "but the father kept on waiting." Two weeks
passed, "but the father kept on waiting." Three weeks
passed, "but the father kept on waiting." Once the refrain
was established, the congregation picked it up and repeated
it every time the preacher did. That's call and response.[6]

My spiritual formation and biformation, as I have previ-
ously stated, took place in churches where people "talked
back" in church. They did it less in St. James Methodist
than in the Baptist and Holiness churches nearby, but my
Methodist forebears did "talk back." If there was any unique
difference between the congregational response, it was that,
while the Methodists tended mostly to "talk back," many of
the neighboring churches had a larger number of people
who seemed also to "preach back." But common to both
was a vocal participation in which we realized that while
only one person had the title "preacher," in truth, it was the
entire church that shared in the preaching. The richness of
the sound was a celebration of the richness of the life in
Christ, the wonder of having life more fully, a wonder
touched off by the hum thought of the preacher.

Participant Proclamation as a Sign
of the Priesthood of All Believers

Although I did not encounter the notion of the priesthood
of all believers until seminary, I intuitively knew about it even
in childhood through the participant proclamation of the congregation. The call and response or the sharing of the procla-

mation of the word by the people, was an effective expression of the priesthood of the entire group in the presence of God.

Like any priestly act, the congregation's response pattern has never been without its critics. I recall that during my spiritual formation in churches where people "talked, felt, and sometimes preached back," some felt that much of it was "off pitch." Much of it, they felt, did not ring true to the gospel or to the claims of those who so vocally shared in it. For example, one of the stated reasons my father gave for supporting my seminary venture was that he hoped it would enable me to do more than "sound empty nothings."

I know now that he was being Pauline in his fatherly way. For he judged that much of what he heard was a "noisy gong and tinkling cymbal" and worst of all "signifying nothing." The charge of "signifying nothing" was a serious indictment in a culture noted for its "signifying ways" of survival. When I said as much to my father, who had only an eighth-grade education, he said his quarrel was not with "signifying," but with "misplaced signifying" in the pulpit at "revivals." With wisdom like that, I wonder whether the father instead of the son may really qualify for a Ph.D.

To illustrate the price he was willing to pay to get me away from "signifying nothings," I must relate what happened the night I left home for Boston University Seminary. The story puts the entire question of call and response into the larger context of how blacks respond to the distortions of American culture. Reading the story, you may glimpse why the freedom of calling and responding in the friendly environment of the church is such a gift, and also why someone like my father would be concerned that the response never become a hollow practice of signifying nothing.

As we stood in front of the railroad station waiting for the 2:00 A.M. Santa Fe train bound for Chicago, where I would change trains for Boston, a tall Caucasian farmer with a long beard and dressed in overalls walked up and asked, "Can you boys give me the time?"

"Boys," I said. "You don't say that to the father of one who has just received a Bachelors degree in Sociology." Then to my father I said, "Dad you look like a man to me."

To my surprise, my father reached for his watch chain, pulled out his watch, and gave the time to the man, who then went on off into the night. What followed amounts to an introduction to practical theology at 2:00 A.M.

Father: "Now, Junior [yes I'm a junior] where are you going?"
Son: "I'm going to Boston to seminary."
Father: "I want you to remember that I'm a World War I veteran and by law permit, have not just one but two guns in the house not to hurt anybody, but to remind the area around us at New Year's when I fire them into the air a couple of times, that I don't want anybody to mess in the wrong way with my family. So I'm not afraid. But where are you going?"
Son: "I'm going to Boston to seminary."

Later, as the old steam engine ran, I could hear my father's words set to the engine's rhythm saying "where are you going, where are you going." I realized then that he put up with some things, not because he liked them or wanted to do them, but so that I would have an opportunity to go away and study. He was not about to jeopardize my opportunities by a response that "signified nothing."

From my perspective many years later I can hear the deeper notes of his response in the train station. I can hear his concern for me, and that concern resonates with the same fullness of sound and life which I heard in the call and response of the congregations that nurtured my spiritual development. For their "amens" undergirded me through my years of young adulthood.

The People's Amen

I pay tribute to those participant listeners when I speak of the "people's Amen." I fear we, as preachers, may take them too much for granted. Their Amen suggests that even in churches where the trend is toward more "feel-back," where the body language is affirmative and the response is deeply felt though unspoken, there may be people who still appreciate those who audibly "talk back," which indicates that this response too is still a vital part of proclamation. Indeed, that may be the way to relate to the churches that still contain aspects of the traditional folk responses in preaching and praise.

In terms of sermon craft, this insight means at least two things. One, we can attend more sensitively to dialogue sermons involving at least two others. Second, we can so craft sermons that they involve the whole congregation in the dialogic experience. Here the preacher, seeking to be faithful to the "priesthood of all people" concept, recognizes and includes co-proclaimers from start to finish in preaching.[7]

As Don Wardlaw says, "Sermon design and rhetoric will reflect [the] indicative stance, envisioning the hearers as co-creators and the response to Scripture, as partners of the Word-event. Listening to God's Word is always a corporate affair."[8]

In summary, let me underscore the point that however central "talk back and preach back" have been in personal congregational spiritual formation, the current trend may be toward a more "feel back" type of response. If that is so, then preaching now should not necessarily be geared toward cultivating a return to the old patterns, because for some they perhaps have had their day. Whatever the case, we are not to assume that participation is waning, or that "feel back" is sufficient in itself to indicate the people's Amen. Instead, we must focus, as Wardlaw says, on developing in both preachers and parishioners a sense of how much the preacher needs the laity's "bold particularity" to remind preachers that they are not gods but persons who themselves need to be spoken to as hearers.[9]

However "bold" the particularity that Wardlaw speaks about, it will be and become "blessed," particularly when the people's Amen sounds and resounds in the assembly. Call and response heightens our understanding that preaching, as Phillips Brooks has said, is truth through personality. But call and response also shows preaching to be more than that. Preaching is truth through *particularity,* the particularity of the hum thought that moves between preacher and congregation as they affirm and celebrate the gospel together.

Chapter 5

FINDING THE PITCH
AND SOUNDING NEW RIFFS

N ow that we have considered the elements of community and consciousness that make up "participant proclamation," let us move closer to the practical ways these are achieved through the preacher's delivery. To accomplish this we need some background information on how the musical elements of pitch and riffs were ignored for many years in the teaching of preaching. If we do not attend to the reasons for their neglect, we may think of them as simply supplemental to the weightier matters of homiletics and fail to recognize their centrality to the practice of preaching as a folk art. We may disparage the mastery of pitch and riffs as ornamental rather than substantive, a kind of "know-how" that people just pick up on their own.

The Neglect of Homiletical Musical Art

Before Craddock (ponder, if you will, the BC resonance in that), "know-how" tended to be an outcast in homiletical teaching and was forced to wander in homeless fashion seeking a home but often refused. I recall when Henry Mitchell encountered this neglect as he began to raise to consciousness the idea of "black preaching." He secured some travel money to visit predominantly black seminaries, but he rarely found welcome mats spread out before him. It seems that several of the deans, many of the faculty, and particularly the teachers of homiletics found troublesome anyone who sought to be too explicit about preaching in the black tradition.

That attitude and response, in part, can be accounted for by what is known in the African American experience as "masking"—hiding the unique character of one's culture or toning it down to avoid being devalued. Masking is a way of surviving, a way of avoiding derision, a way of appearing more acceptable to the dominant ethos.

Take special note of the phrase "African American," which is currently being used more deliberately than "black" or the abbreviated "Afro." This new name affirms the raised awareness and consciousness we possess, and is the resulting legacy of the most recent stage of the civil rights movement. It is a way of moving beyond masking to claim one's identity without apology. Apparently, what was once asserted under the banner of "black power" is now being incorporated under the designation and action of "bold particularity." This phrase, as we saw in the last chapter, is used by Don Wardlaw in his discussion of the corporate role shared by both parishioner and preacher in gospel proclamation or participant proclamation.[1] I find it liberating to discover this common ground and to realize that our struggle to declare ourselves partners in American pluralism is akin to our struggle to realize the extent to which we are, in Reuel Howe's words, "partners in preaching."[2]

Perhaps it was some failure to see this common ground—or some wariness about it when it was seen—that accounted for the cold reception Henry Mitchell received in his first attempts to assess the extent to which seminaries included the black tradition's insights in teaching and practicing preaching. I count myself among the few who welcomed him but must confess that I too had a lot of "unlearning" to do about homiletics and preaching.

What I had to unlearn, however, was not primarily a matter of content but more a matter of context, the assumptions and ethos that were a part of teaching homiletics in an academic setting. No one forced me to promulgate a particular approach to preaching; no one said the class had to favor a homiletic that stressed one-way communication from the pulpit to the pew; or that I had to neglect the musical elements of preaching as a folk art. It was more complex than that.

What I realized was that even though I intuitively felt black communal preaching possibilities, I had not, within myself, allowed them to become a conscious art. At that time there was virtually no literature, especially homiletical literature, to spark my particular interest. But more than that, there were very few writers in the homiletical field who acknowledged black pulpit elements except for an occasional humorous reference to the black preachers who said, "First, I tells them what I am going to tell them, then I tells them, and finally, I tells them what I told them." This was about all that existed at the time.

Of course, we know by now that this was just another way of acknowledging the "rationalistic captivity" of the sermon. That may be a rather harsh way of putting it, for there are still serious advocates and practitioners of the deductive sermon. I put it that way not so much to quarrel with those advocates but to dramatize the fact that the "folk" aspects as a whole, not only the "black experience in preaching and praise," were left out.

It seems that being left out was so pervasive in the African American's experience that "masking" became a way of life. Ralph Ellison, the African American novelist and critic cited earlier, used the word "invisible" and developed it into a powerful narrative account that portrays the unique manner in which black people have incarnated a human experience. His novel *Invisible Man* partakes of symbols that resound universally and speak to the human spirit while at the same time they show the masking which was operating in the homiletics classroom.[3]

It is no wonder, therefore, that in this context, several theological seminaries felt uneasy about Henry Mitchell's inquiry and research. It was not that they were entirely blind or deaf to the resonances of the black preaching tradition for all people. They were, perhaps, unsure about exactly what they had "masked" in order to survive as a people. This left them uncertain and guarded as a church about openly submitting to research about their homiletics, even though the inquirer was also an African American.

Maybe the hesitancy to welcome someone who sought to be explicit about preaching in the black tradition, was due to the low status orality has fallen to in a print-oriented world. Homiletics had reached a place where content reigned supreme over the preaching venture. The script had become primary to the Spirit, and print had become lord over plot and even proclamation itself—or so it seemed.

Eugene Lowry developed a formula to recover the element of "plot" in preaching. His work, *The Homiletical Plot,* made available to the discipline of preaching recent reflections on the narrative aspects on experience in literature and theology.[4] He demonstrated how the pulpit could employ the insights numerous scholars such as Amos Wilder had discovered in biblical literature, particularly insights about the role of narrative in proclaiming the gospel. However, as much as preachers needed to recall the central role of plot in preaching, we also needed to recognize the extent to which preaching as an oral medium requires and depends on oral delivery. It is in recognition of that fact that I seek to add my reflections on sermon pitch.

I realize that I have provided a long introduction to the subject of this chapter, finding the pitch and sounding new riffs. But this introduction is integral to what is involved; it is essential to establish the setting in which pitch and riffs are considered. Henry Mitchell's story reveals how the black preaching tradition has been neglected by both whites and blacks. Upon realizing this, you can appreciate the fact that what I am saying is not for blacks only; nor is it aimed at whites only. All have hesitated to treat these musical homiletical elements seriously, and all have the potential to employ them in their own way as participant proclaimers.

The Characteristics of Sermonic Pitch

When we think of pitch in music, the simplest meaning that comes to mind is the tone of a particular wave frequency, such as when the oboist plays an A of 440 for the orchestra to tune to. But pitch is actually more complex than this. Gifted instrumentalists and singers vary the vibrato, intensity, dynamics, and coloring of their tone so that there is a complex character to the sound. If we turn on the radio and hear a favorite singer or musician, we can usually identify the person immediately—this one slides off the pure pitch in a way that suggests a broken heart, or that one uses a wide vibrato that sends a beat into the air, and so forth.

Not only do these different treatments of pitch characterize individual performers, they also reflect various musical idioms. For example, a concert singer ornamenting an aria from Handel's *Messiah* may strive to keep the pitch right on center of each note, while a blues singer will deliberately slide through several notes. Our ears pick up the dramatic difference and we recognize each as typical of that particular style of music.

Music does not all sound the same, nor does preaching. There is a particular sound, a particular pitch to various homiletical traditions, and this pitch is no small matter. If it is not sounded in a way that is "in tune" with the community's ear and heart, then the congregation will be no more responsive than concert goers who are expecting an evening of blues, but find they have walked into a festival on Handel.

I owe much of my appreciation for the importance of sermon pitch to James Massey, a New Testament teacher and parish and university preacher, who realized how integral sermon delivery is to the theological and communicative substance of the black preaching tradition. I was intrigued that, as a scholar, he gave such serious attention to delivery as more than simply a homiletical "how-to." After many discussions with him, I admit that I am perhaps making more of this than he intended. At any rate, I find that his list of the characteristics of the black homiletical tradition helps to refine my understanding of the distinctive pitch of African American participant proclamation. These characteristics help us hear the pitch that the congregation finds in tune with its expectations and needs.

First, says Massey, black preaching is *functional*. It is done for the people's, the hearer's sake. Experiencing the sermon is valued over and above any material uses and implications which may be derived. This reflects perhaps, the West African sensibility where art and artifices are not "museum centered" but "meaning centered," quite the opposite of that of most Westerners. Only in recent years, since tourism has highlighted their commercial appeal to outsiders, have the art and artifices of the more "folk-oriented" communities of the world become more "money-oriented" than "meaning-centered."

The second characteristic of the black tradition Massey lists is that preaching is *festive*. It majors in the celebrative aspects of faith even as it sings of the troubles nobody knows. This is a point shared with all who have been victimized, and when Du Bois speaks of Negro or black spirituals as "sorrow songs," he is putting a finger on what is common in the Psalms as well as in other expressions from the downtrodden. When black worshipers say, "Help 'em Lord!" they may be in spiritual pain but still be festive enough to suggest that the preacher needs help to match the message with the mood. Invoking the Lord's help, for example, was once very much a common utterance for those preachers who tried to preach funeral services. Although that practice has long since ceased, the half humorous "Help 'em Lord!" response is a plea to keep mood and message appropriate to the occasion. The problem in recognizing the humor is that it tends easily to distract from the hurt that is very much a part of the total experience—hurts which the blues tradition expresses as "laughing to keep from crying." This concept is much more profound than I am able to outline here, but it sufficiently suggests the "trouble-glory" mixture in black praise.

Festivity comes to the preaching craft more in terms of context than content. It is part of the congregation's orientation, a predisposition that they bring to the hearing of sermons, and provides a heightened sensitivity to the festive element that is already present in biblical stories.

There are traces of this festive element in the evaluative form that I discussed in chapter 1. The "folk" liturgical expressions "Help 'em Lord!" "Well?" and "That's all right!" are spoken by the congregation with an air of celebration. In offering these responses the people are helping the preacher to lead the entire congregation into the corporate act of celebrating God's word.

This is truly an aspect of the black preaching tradition where the participant dimension of proclamation is clearly evident. The freedom to express oneself amounts to what can be called "congregational punctuation" and indicates that while the preacher can initiate a pace, it is not the preacher's alone. The hearer has a part in it as well. Even when there is a congregation that feels back more than it talks back, the very willingness to recognize the part the hearer plays in the proclamation is often enough to maintain the pitch on a level that keeps faith sweet and strong.

Third, the sermon pitch also reveals that black preaching is *communal*. The pitch belongs not to the preacher alone but to the congregation as well. This is a key characteristic supporting the claim for participant proclamation because it exposes the extent to which the whole church or congregation preaches. Once this is realized, the individualism that so easily besets us is dispelled. The community's understanding that preaching is a communal act gives brother Ward's Amen a chance to sound (see chapter 3, "The People's Amen" section). It allows those who "talk back" and those who "feel back" to know they are accepted and not merely tolerated. All members of the congregation are given a place in the sermon to respond as the Spirit moves them, whether aloud or in silence, whether with a gesture or by sitting still.

The fourth characteristic of African American sermon pitch is its *radical* nature. "Radical" here means it goes to the roots of the black experience. The preaching boldly discusses the particularity of the people and their distinctive lives, and draws upon the primal vision and voice of the black consciousness. Claiming the full context of the African American experience, the voice of the preacher is freed to encompass the entire range of tonal expression. It is not a Lone Ranger voice; it is a communal voice and can sound life's laments and its laughter, its grief and its glory. "Radical" also means that the participant proclaimers are open to resound freedom in all of its varieties and especially to resound the "harmonies of liberty."

Martin Luther King, Jr., nurtured this radicalness. It was not reckless but responsible. King became a living embodiment of what his major professor in graduate school, Lynn Harold DeWolf, discussed in his book *Responsible Freedom*.[5] Thus the pitch of the sermon, the way the full sorrow and yearning of black people sounded in King's voice, was more than a rhetorical strategy. It was a witness to an ethical stance, an exercise of freedom in a way that was responsive to the rightful demands for justice and equality. The pitch of his preaching matched the pitch in the hearts of the people, thereby giving them power to act for what was right and fair.

To be sure, many have chosen and still choose the more conservative option, but the fact that anybody chooses the radical option in a racist society is a marvel that can only be credited to God. For the radical quality of the true homiletical pitch originates not just in the human heart but in the music of heaven.

The fifth and final characteristic that sermon pitch reveals is that black preaching is *climactic.* Sermon delivery is a creative and inclusive moment where the preacher embodies for the whole congregation or group of hearers their celebrative gifts. It is a time when all that has been generative in the pulpit, pew, or elsewhere is seen as organic to life. What results is not far from chant. Indeed, in my classes that are held during the Fall semester, I set as a central goal that by Thanksgiving the students will be able not only to count their blessings but also to chant them. In some circles this is called "whooping," where meter and message not only meet but celebrate. It may mean different styles for different people. I find that the chant or liturgical chanting is a common ground ecumenically in which to explore the preaching possibilities discussed here.

Pitch, then, illustrates how essential delivery is to black preaching. The sound of the sermon is not simply something added to the substance but rather is inseparable from the experience of participant proclamation, which is a communal event in the life of the congregation. Pitch is an essential element of "homiletical musicality," and when the true pitch is combined with new riffs, then preaching takes on an extraordinary vitality.

Other Sources of Homiletical Pitch

Having identified this communal character of pitch in the black preaching tradition, I want to stress that it is not limited to African Americans. There are resources in other traditions that can encourage this communal dimension of homiletical pitch. For example, when a congregation shares in biblical reflection on the lessons from a lectionary, then what Wardlaw terms "social contextuality" embraces both laity and preacher, and the pitch of the sermon has a sound that the community recognizes as authentic and empowering. Even if they are only feeling back and not talking back, the people are equipped to join in the proclamation.

Sound On: New Riffs for <u>God's Trombones</u>

When James Weldon Johnson consciously sought to capture the essence of the preaching tradition of his forebears, he had to try to put something that was essentially oral into written form. His problem was how to write what was once only spoken. His literary achievement is titled *God's Trombones*.

Trombones was his way of putting into a Negro verse some of the tried-and-true sermons that are preached and are loved by black folk and the black Christian tradition. His effort was experimental, something that should be extended and refined and elaborated on by what the "blues" musician calls "riffs," a designation for the beat, either of a single musical instrument or of a band, when the text does not last for a full musical phrase and must be continued. It is characterized by improvised free rhythms and idiomatic counterpoint, which make for a style that is difficult to notate since it depends upon the experience, tradition, and sensitivity of the performer.[6]

The improvisory and anticipatory aspects of "riff" can be

extended and broadened as a metaphor to illumine several aspects that embrace the call-and-response relationship of laity and preacher in the black tradition. I hear at least three riffs in this tradition. These riffs allow me to repeat some of my earlier points but now in a new tone.

The first riff would be in the area of prayer. Certainly much can be made of the role of the laity in the beginning prayer of *God's Trombones* and the confessional stance indicated in the phrase "empty pitchers before a full count." The current increased role of the laity in the life of the church marks a more conscious role as participant proclaimers. Moreover, the petitions to "hitch to the wisdom post" and "turpentine the imagination" can, given the current ferment theologically, hermeneutically, and homiletically in theology and liturgy, make for some new riffs for proclamation. Every time preachers touch upon the prayers of the congregation, from petitions spoken aloud to the sighs too deep for words, they are sounding a prayer riff, a variation on the yearnings of the hearts of their people.

In the black worship and praise tradition, there are numerous prayer legacies. They range from thanking God for "having one more chance to be out to the house of worship" to "keeping our couch from becoming our tomb—or our cooling board." The tradition includes the confession that we are "like empty pitchers before a full fount." All of these are prayers that resound from our yesterdays. Their substance and spirit however are finding new and relevant wording, such as that of M. L. Harvey in *Prayer in the Black Tradition,* who prays: "We bring ourselves to attention in Thy presence, Eternal Father, as those who find in Thee the whence and why and whither of their lives."[7]

The second riff would be what a recent exegete of 1 and 2 Kings calls "pausal" moments in the Deuteronomic redactor's appropriation of the biblical tradition wherein his editorial and theological vision is articulated. That pausal moment is a time for filling, indeed fulfilling, with content what would otherwise be a mere dramatic break in style and delivery. Burke O. Long, in his commentary on 1 Kings, speaks of the "pausal moments" which are to be filled with matters of thematic importance, allowing the author-editor opportunity to present "a theological commentary on the fate of Israel."[8]

You can hear such riffs in black preaching when the preacher, who has been spinning out the narrative line of the biblical story, comes to a point where the story has piled up upon itself, for a moment the telling stops, and the congregation's response decrescendos. The preacher applies a rest to the momentum, and then repeats a word several times, a word that soon leads into a theological reflection on the meaning of all that has preceded. That pause and the reflection that follows constitute a homiletical riff, a stretched-out rhythm elaborated into sermonic richness.

The third riff embraces the wide range of tonal inflections that characterize the black preaching tradition. These inflections can vary enormously through the course of a single sermon; from the reflective tone of pausal moments, to a voice filled with the sorrow and suffering of the community, to righteous anger at injustice, to the celebratory music of faith and hope. These riffs arise from being an oral culture. Yet more than this, they represent the development of a sophisticated expressive palette that allowed black preachers to give full vent to the experience of their people when the surrounding Western society was restraining them.

Although the origins of these riffs may be traced to oppressive conditions, we can count these riffs as blessings in light of the distortions that strict rationality has inflicted upon the consciousness and sensibilities of the West. It just may be that in this day of global awareness, the riffs of black preaching can be a vehicle of the Spirit working to revitalize what Walter Ong has called the basic oral noetic. That is to say, the riffs of prayer, pause, and inflection as practiced by black preachers may help those beyond the African American community to hear the deepest pleadings of the human heart for justice and compassion. Whenever this happens, whenever the rich homiletic of African American communities mobilizes energies for the transformation of society, then the music of God's trombones moves beyond the church's walls and renews the world with the pitch and the riffs of the Spirit sounding in daily life.

Chapter 6

FINDING THE BRIDGES BETWEEN OUR VOICE AND THE COMMUNITY'S

*T*he current narrative emphasis in preaching is revealing the extent to which homiletics has long been oriented to Greek and rationalistic forms and approaches. Hans Frei made this clear in his book *The Eclipse of Biblical Narrative,* and the dialogue between theologians and literary critics has made narrative and story more central in preaching particularly, and in theology as a whole.[1] We have now reached the point where the initial excitement and bit of faddism in story preaching are giving way to a more self-critical stage. Michael Goldberg made an exhaustive study of narrative in theology and proposed three criteria for interpreting and employing the use of narrative in preaching:

1. Do not use narrative for hidden philosophical views.
2. Identify the various narrative genres and use them correctly.
3. Understand the communal context of narrative, since, if it is to be effective, it must relate to far more than the preacher's personal story.[2]

It is the last of these critical criteria, the communal context, that has sparked my interest in the folk art aspects of preaching. For folk art is the expression not simply of an isolated artistic self, but of the broader experiences and values of the group.

The Special Qualities of Oral Culture

I stress particularly the oral aspect of folk life rather than the variety of cultural idiosyncrasies. Historically, the term "folk" has referred to the customs and values that have characterized a particular people's lifestyle and manner of doing things. "Folk art" in literature centers on the oral manner in which a people communicate and by which they develop their unique customs of seeing and knowing. Such cultures receive notice especially for the ways they form and transmit their history and carry on their day-to-day affairs. Folk culture is often contrasted with print-oriented cultures where reading and writing achieve dominance.

My interest in the folk aspects of preaching surfaced when I sought to teach a primarily oral tradition in an academic, print-oriented setting. The contrast of tradition and context was revealing. The high value placed on orality by the tradition was amplified in the act of preaching since the sermon is above all an oral medium. The folk tendencies of the tradition had been kept vital and alive in the face of the segregation and subordination of black people, a phenomenon found in other communities as well.

Meanwhile, the academic setting, true to its own ethos and values, had kept vital and alive the values of written communication and scholarly discourse.

Thus, oral and print cultures came together in my class, and the contrasts between the two highlighted for me the distinctive ways in which preachers, depending on their traditions, forge bridges between themselves and their communities. I found myself having to formulate an approach to preaching that would deal with the tensions of people learning homiletics in a formal class when their calling was to preach in a communal context whose distinctive character was different from that of academia.

I was helped in this task by Bruce Rosenberg's book, *The Art of the American Folk Preacher*.[3] He made me aware of the uniquely American aspects of folk preaching and took note that it embraced not only American blacks but also some Appalachian whites. The latter was a surprise, but brought to mind some of the questions I shared with instructors who taught preaching in or near Appalachian communities. The parallelism of our homiletical concerns revealed that what I was dealing with was not limited to the African American community. I was encountering a basic issue of how preacher, sermon, and community are all bridged together in oral culture.

I discovered that the way Bruce Rosenberg came to his research is similar to how James Weldon Johnson arrived at his decision to experiment in Negro verse in *God's Trombones*.[4] At the time, Rosenberg was a graduate student in medieval literature at Ohio University. One day he was about to switch off a black urban radio preacher when he recognized some oral features that were similar to those of the singers in Homer and in the English "Canterbury Tales" and "Beowulf." It was a recognition that was strong enough to suggest a problem for his dissertation and writings. It caused him to concentrate especially on the residues of that oral tradition and those oral singers who were still extant in America.

In a similar fashion James Weldon Johnson came to his experiments in Negro or black verse especially in preaching, when, after a very busy day on the NAACP circuit, he settled down for an anticipated long church service only to be enthralled by a narrative-oriented black preacher reciting the Creation narrative. Something in the delivery reminded

Johnson of the sermons he had heard in his youth. He remembers being so excited that in spite of his weariness he jotted down some notes, which in time became what we know as the "Creation." Johnson decided then and there to try to recapture the genius of the old black preachers.

Although his undertaking was more self-consciously literary and less oral than Rosenberg's research, the result was that Johnson provided suggestive insights about the act and the art of black preaching and indeed of folk preaching in general.

What I invite you to share now, however, deals less with the experiments he then labeled as "Negro verse" and more with the choices and options he discusses in his preface, which provides the principles for what I call the preacher's "folk work."

The Dilemma of Oral Dialect in Print Culture

Johnson says that his desire to recapture the old-time black preaching confronted him with a dilemma about dialect. Since his approach was basically literary, should he reconstruct the sermons in the "dis and dats" of so-called Negro speech? Or should he express them in a language more fitting to the sacredness of the medium and the solemnity of the message? He decided against using dialect in the manner of Paul Laurence Dunbar because it was limited to minstrelsy and pathos, which were too narrow for the preaching tradition he sought to recapture.[5]

Johnson felt that neither minstrelsy nor pathos was fitting for the grandeur of the preachers or their message, because their speech and language in the pulpit was different from the kind they spoke elsewhere. In the pulpit they spoke not dialect, but "biblical language" because many of them, though forbidden to read, had memorized lengthy passages of the King James Version of the Bible. What they actually spoke, he says, was not slave English or Black English. It was biblical English. So he chose biblical rather than Black English.

In doing this Johnson revealed something about the nature of the folk preacher, especially a conception of preaching that indicated the preacher felt called to make use of the grandest language available to proclaim the word.

This decision for an elegant biblical style speaks to those who would limit the black idiom to what has been called "Black English." Quite contrary to the early emphasis of Henry Mitchell's work, which advocated the use of Black English,[6] the decision of Johnson to use biblical language illumines his concern to avoid an ideological portrayal of Negro or black life and thought. I believe Johnson's responsiveness to the folk tradition's sensitivity to language is worth noting and maintaining. It has been a rhetorical strategy of the folk tradition that has helped the word to resound with dignity and power, forging one of the vital oral bridges between preacher, sermon, and community.

The Context Factor in Dialect Decisions

Johnson's precision in identifying the biblical character of the black folk preacher's language does not preclude his appreciation for the distinctive style of black dialect. I find I resonate with his theory about that form of expression. He says there is nothing inherently wrong with black dialect, but using it is a matter of overall context. Rather than make an ideological judgment for or against such speech, consider how it will be heard and received in a particular setting. This contextual understanding helps conserve the folk aspects of our heritage while at the same time we avoid condemning our folkways just because they have been abused. Whether Johnson would feel that black dialect can be freely used today, we can only guess. There still lingers that tendency to stereotype what is not ours, and perhaps Johnson would still find black dialect closer to the minstrelsy side. One thing is sure, he would not refuse any black idiom as something of which to be ashamed. His aim would be to be true to the nature of the communal integrity one is called to portray.

I believe the subtlety and complexity of Johnson's position on black dialect illumine what I mean by the bridges between preacher, sermon, and community. I am using his discussion to help us see that these links are not a function of the preacher's language in isolation. Just as Johnson, as a literary artist, had to consider how he would convey the power and eloquence of black preaching without stereotyping it, so preachers have to make decisions about their language in light of their communal context. A simple decision for or against this or that idiom is not adequate. The preacher has to decide how his or her language will help in forging the bridge that links preacher, sermon, and community, the sense of a shared proclamation and celebration of the gospel.

What is appropriate under one set of circumstances may not be in another. This is part of the dynamic and shifting nature of oral culture. Sometimes members of a minority group may attempt to establish contact with the dominant culture, and sometimes deliberately they seek a contrasting idiom, a realm of discourse that gives free play to the community's distinctive identity and expression.

One way for preachers to appropriate James Weldon Johnson's reflections on the complexity of using dialect is through what I have called "folk work." I mean by this term, consciously addressing the way our language as preachers has been shaped by the oral culture that has raised us and understanding how our idiom must vary according to the forces that characterize the particular communal context in which we preach. Indeed, I suggest "folk work" as an assignment for all my preaching students who come from a predominantly oral culture. For every ethnic group has to discover how to appropriate its heritage, especially in the pluralistic context that is America. This is because, as we noted earlier, all of us who share ethnic heritages with the nation have what Du Bois called a sense of twoness or a double-mindedness, living as we do as minorities in American society.

Folk Work for Minorities and the Dominant Culture

I do not believe the task of folk work should be limited to minorities however. It would be helpful to those from the dominant culture to consider these issues as well. Folk work would make them aware of at least two things:

1. the assumptions and values that permeate their preaching as members of the reigning culture
2. the special burden of communication that rests upon minority preachers who are having to communicate with their own people while maintaining bridges to the dominant systems of power and value

For example, one folk work assignment for a person from the mainstream could be to try to discover how they can grasp and appreciate another preaching tradition without disowning their own heritage and trying to be blacker than "thou" or more Hispanic than thou and so on.

These folk work assignments can be extended to regional areas. A case in point would be working to overcome the communications breakdown Liston Pope spoke about years ago in *Millhands and Preachers*.[7] He traced the gap that emerged for Southern seminarians, who left home to pursue theological study in the North, only to find that their education made it difficult for them to identify with their home churches. This is an extension of Johnson's suggestion, but it is an instance of how folk aspects of preaching can be utilized to enhance the pulpit and the practice of preaching.

An Ear Attuned to the People

In my own teaching at the Howard Divinity School, we have attempted to draw the folk aspects of preaching into the formal teaching of homiletics through the responsive evaluation form presented earlier:

1. Help 'em Lord!
2. Well?
3. That's all right!
4. Amen!
5. Glory Hallelujah!

This form of evaluation helps to elicit from the class an awareness of the oral bridges, the connective dynamics between preacher, sermon, and community. It takes seriously the critical homiletical capacities of the congregation as they are expressed in and through the oral traditions of "folk art" preaching. These critical capacities are not reserved for a judgment about the sermon that will be made upon its conclusion. Rather they are part of the community's corporate work with the preacher to make the sermon a shared event.

For a preacher to lead the people in such an event requires the kind of sensibilities James Weldon Johnson displays in *God's Trombones*. It takes a good ear, a homiletical ear to work with folk idioms, an ear attuned to the people. That preacher's ear, that deep sense of matching sound and sense to the shared sound and sense of the community, is one of the keys of preaching in an oral culture.

The Bridge Between Image and Story

However, the ear alone is not sufficient. Just as I have
been exploring the relationship between idiom and narrative, I believe there is another vital bridge between image
and story, a link maintained with great artistry throughout
God's Trombones. Richard Eslinger in *A New Hearing* criti-
cally examines the work of preachers oriented to story and
inductive homiletic, including Fred Craddock, Henry
Mitchell, Eugene Lowry, Charles Rice, and David Buttrick.[8]
Among these preachers, Buttrick is the only one who
attempts to probe the relationship between narrative and
image. The rest still have traces of the "main idea" or topical
element in preaching and sermon crafting. Thus their narrative is liable to lose the idiomatic expression that we have
been exploring here.

The biblical English that Johnson chooses and employs in
his own writing grows primarily out of the images of Scripture, not out of theological topics or statements. This is not
to say that there is not a theological dimension to the writing, but rather that its theological insight arises primarily
from image and story, and where and how they intersect.

This is not a less demanding form of thought and expression than reasoning through concepts, but it is different in
character. It can be done poorly or well, just as thinking in
concepts can be done poorly or well. There are images that
convey meaning by their appropriateness and power, and
others that do not, just as there are logical constructions
that strike us as sound, and others that appear to represent
faulty reasoning.

I believe folk work involves the rigorous discipline of
learning to think of and express the gospel through images
and story by artfully interweaving the two. As preachers do
this they are drawing upon the bridges between themselves
and the community in a way that makes the participant
proclamation an event of corporate meaning.

Bridges That Build the Church

Finding bridges is more than a homiletical method. Although it involves artistry and discipline, it is in the last analysis the way the church is built up as a community of believers. The bridges are homiletical realities that manifest the relationship between the people, their sacred story, and the living Spirit in their midst.

When the people say, "Help 'em Lord!" they are in part saying, "O Lord, help the preacher find the bridges of meaning, Spirit, grace, and faith that hold us together and connect us to you." When they say, "That's all right!" they are saying, "You're getting there, Preacher, you're finding those connections that we need." And when they exclaim, "Glory Hallelujah!" they are expressing the joy of feeling with all their heart that the Spirit has worked through the preacher and themselves to bring them into the joyful, redemptive presence of God.

Notes

Chapter 1: Homiletical Musicality from "Help 'em Lord" to "Glory Hallelujah!"

1. The description discussed by William C. Turner, Jr., "The Musicality of Black Preaching: A Phenomenology," *The Journal of Black Sacred Music,* vol. 2, no. 1 (Spring 1988): 27.
2. Abraham Joshua Heschel, *The Sabbath: Its Meaning for Modern Man* (New York: H. Wolff, 1951), p. 8.
3. See the discussions in Howard Thurman, *The Creative Encounter* (New York: Harper and Row, 1954); *The Search for Common Ground: An Inquiry into the Basis of Man's Experience of Community* (New York: Harper and Row, 1971); and *The Luminous Darkness: A Personal Interpretation of the Anatomy of Segregation and the Ground of Hope* (New York: Harper and Row, 1965).
4. Michael Kammen, *People of Paradox* (New York: Vintage, 1973), chapter 4, pp. 97ff.
5. The phrase is Melvin Seeman's, "Intellectual Perspectives and Adjustments to Minority Status," *Social Problems* 4 (January 1956): 142-53.
6. Janheinz Jahn, *Muntu: An Outline of the New African Culture* (New York: Grove Press, 1961).
7. Clearly Massey and Forbes lift up spirituality in their view of black preaching. In my view Massey does it most helpfully by discussing it under the general terms of delivery. But Forbes does it most completely by keeping the transcendental element central with his focus on "anointing." This puts the polishing of craft and technique in its

proper place. The refinement of our art is not the final goal of preaching but is one of the means of fulfilling what we have been called to do. See discussions in James Earl Massey, *Designing the Sermon* (Nashville: Abingdon, 1980), and *The Responsible Pulpit* (Anderson, Ind.: Warner Press, 1974); James Forbes, *The Holy Spirit and Preaching* (Nashville: Abingdon Press, 1989).

Henry Mitchell's works and writings in the perspective of the "itys" seem more akin to the "truth through particularity" emphasis. There is a folk-oriented aspect of his discussions that seems to justify this placement. His utilization of Eliade's concept of "transconsciousness" suggests that this placement must not be too rigid, for it allows him to put insights on preaching in a way that can be informed by the history of religion rather than by some narrow parochial and cultural view. See Henry H. Mitchell, *Black Preaching: The Recovery of a Powerful Art* (Nashville: Abingdon Press, 1990), and *Celebration and Experience in Preaching* (Nashville: Abingdon Press, 1990).

Cornel West has a brief discussion of the black preacher and preaching that is insightful because it is set in the context of a theological analysis of culture. As a possible continuation of what I call the Duboisian critique, which seeks to hold in tension what is American and what is African, West has some analytical categories that inform preaching as a whole. His brief comments seem also to echo some of the aesthetic insights of Ralph Ellison and Langston Hughes. See Cornel West, *Prophetic Fragments* (Grand Rapids: Wm. B. Eerdmans Publishing Co., 1988), pp. 42-45.

The musicality features of black preaching are discussed by Jon Michael Spenser in *Sacred Symphony: The Chanted Sermon of the Black Preacher* (Westport, Conn.: Greenwood, 1987). Spenser attempts to note how black preaching appropriates what I call "musical" features of its tradition for embellishments and enhancement. Gerald Davis in *I Got the Word in Me and I Can Sing It You Know* (Philadelphia: University of Pennsylvania Press, 1985), has some helpful insights on black preaching derived from his discoveries and critiques of the Epic Singer tradition.

8. Spenser, *Sacred Symphony,* and *Protest and Praise: Sacred Music of Black Religion* (Minneapolis: Fortress Press, 1990).

9. James Weldon Johnson, *God's Trombones* (New York: Viking Press, 1927).

10. See Vernon J. Dixon and Badi Foster, eds., *Beyond Black or White: An Alternate America* (Boston: Little, Brown & Co., 1971), chap. 3, pp. 48-66. There are suggestions for a critical and creative hermeneutic in their discussion and analyses.

NOTES

Chapter 2: Sermon Pause: Setting the Climate for Participation

1. Fred B. Craddock, *Preaching* (Nashville: Abingdon Press, 1985), pp. 52-53.
2. Erik Erikson, *Childhood and Society,* quoted in Michael Kammen, *People of Paradox* (New York: Vintage, 1972). See chap. 4, "Biformity: A Frame of Reference," pp. 97-116.
3. W. E. B. Du Bois, *The Souls of Black Folk* (Chicago: A. C. M. McClurg, 1907), p. 4.
4. See discussion in Vernon J. Dixon and Badi Foster, *Beyond Black or White* (Boston: Little, Brown & Co., 1971) and in Kimberly W. Benston, ed., *Speaking for You: The Vision of Ralph Ellison* (Washington, D.C.: Howard University Press, 1987).
5. Thomas Long, "Plotting the Text's Claim Upon Us," in Don Wardlaw, ed., *Preaching Biblically: Creating Sermons in the Shape of Scripture* (Philadelphia: Westminster Press, 1983), p. 86.
6. Ibid., p. 87; and Eugene Lowry, *Doing Time in the Pulpit* (Nashville: Abingdon Press, 1985), pp. 7-8.
7. Abraham Joshua Heschel, *The Sabbath: Its Meaning for Modern Man* (New York: H. Wolff, 1951), p. 99.
8. Lowry, *Doing Time in the Pulpit.* See chapter 1, "Sermon Time as the Ordering of Experience," pp. 11-28.
9. John Greenleaf Whittier, "Dear Lord and Father of Mankind."
10. See Bruce C. Salmon, *Storytelling in Preaching: A Guide to Theory and Practice* (Nashville: Broadman Press, 1988), p. 56.
11. Burke O. Long, *I Kings with an Introduction to Historical Literature,* ed. Rolf Knierim and Gene M. Tucker, *The Forms of the Old Testament Literature,* vol. 9 (Grand Rapids: Wm. B. Eerdmans Publishing Co., 1984), pp. 25-30.

Chapter 3: Resounding the People's Amen

1. Bruce Rosenberg, *The Art of the American Folk Preacher* (New York: Oxford University Press, 1970).
2. Fred B. Craddock, *Preaching* (Nashville: Abingdon Press, 1985).
3. George W. Swank, *Dialogic Style in Preaching* (Valley Forge, Pa.: Judson Press, 1981).
4. "Praise to the Lord! The Almighty, the King of Creation!" words by Joachim Neander, trans. Catherine Winkworth, in Erik Routley, *A Panorama of Christian Hymnody* (Chicago: G.I.A. Publications, 1979), p. 91.
5. Leander E. Keck, *The Bible in the Pulpit* (Nashville: Abingdon, 1978), pp. 53-54.

6. Ibid., p. 40.
7. Don M. Wardlaw, "Preaching as the Interface of Two Social Worlds," in Arthur Van Seters, ed., *Preaching as a Social Act* (Nashville: Abingdon Press, 1988), p. 62.
8. William D. Thompson, *Preaching Biblically: Exegesis and Interpretation* (Nashville: Abingdon, 1981), pp. 20-21.
9. Dieter T. Hessel, *Social Themes of the Christian Year: A Commentary on the Lectionary* (Philadelphia: Geneva Press, 1983).
10. Wardlaw, "Preaching as the Interface," pp. 55-84.
11. Gardner C. Taylor, *How Shall They Preach* (Elgin, Ill.: Progressive Baptist Publishing House, 1977), p. 60: "Altogether too much preaching, particularly in what are called the mainline churches, is too flat, too horizontal, too colorless, too unimaginative."
12. Wardlaw, "Preaching as the Interface," p. 58.
13. Fanny J. Crosby, "Blessed Assurance, Jesus Is Mine."
14. Craddock, *Preaching,* pp. 52-65.
15. "For the Beauty of the Earth," words by Folliot S. Pierpoint.

Chapter 4: Hum Thought: Tales, Tunes, and Talk

1. Ralph Ellison, *Invisible Man* (New York: Random House, 1952).
2. Dwight Stevenson and Charles Diehl, *Reaching People from the Pulpit: A Guide to Effective Sermon Delivery* (New York: Harper and Row, 1958), pp. 148-52.
3. See definition and discussion of this phrase in Vernon J. Dixon and Badi Foster, *Beyond Black or White: An Alternate America* (Boston: Little, Brown & Co., 1971). "Diunital is a neologism constructed in the following manner. Webster tells us that *di* means 'akin to two' or 'apart.' Unital, the adjectival form of the word *unit* means a 'single thing that constitutes an undivided whole.' Diunital, therefore, is literally something apart and united at the same time," n. 4, p. 26. This can be extended to formulations like "Wounded Healer" (Nouwen), "Luminous Darkness" (Thurman), and "responsible freedom" (DeWolf). It can be extended to Michael Kammen's *People of Paradox: An Inquiry Concerning the Origins of American Civilization* (New York: Vintage Books, 1972). In a chapter entitled "Biformity: A Frame of Reference," he quotes from Erik H. Erikson's insight in *Childhood and Society* (1950): "It is commonplace to state that whatever one may come to consider as truly American can be shown to have its equally characteristic opposite. This, one suspects, is true of all 'national characters' or (as I would prefer to call them) national identities—so true,

in fact, that one may begin rather than end with the proposition that a nation's identity is derived from the ways in which history has, as it were, counterpointed; the ways in which it lifts this counterpoint to a unique style of civilization, or lets it disintegrate into mere contradiction," p. 97.

4. Lynn Harold DeWolf, *Responsible Freedom: Guidelines to Christian Action* (New York: Harpers, 1971).
5. Phillips Brooks, *Lectures on Preaching* (New York: E. P. Dutton, 1877 [Seabury Press, 1964]).
6. Wyatt T. Walker, "Song, Sermon, and the Spoken Word," in *Sagala: A Journal of Art and Ideas* (Summer 1980): 18.
7. See George W. Swank's appropriation and discussion of current trends in homiletics in his brief but helpful book *Dialogic Style in Preaching* (Valley Forge, Pa.: Judson Press, 1981).
8. Don M. Wardlaw, "Preaching as the Interface of Two Social Worlds," in Arthur Van Seters, ed., *Preaching as a Social Act* (Nashville: Abingdon Press, 1988), pp. 62, 65.
9. Ibid., p. 68.

Chapter 5: Finding the Pitch and Sounding New Riffs

1. Don M. Wardlaw, "Preaching as the Interface of Two Social Worlds" in Arthur Van Seters, ed., *Preaching as a Social Act* (Nashville: Abingdon Press, 1988), pp. 67-69.
2. Reuel L. Howe, *Partners in Preaching* (New York: Seabury Press, 1967).
3. Ralph Ellison, *Invisible Man* (New York: Random House, 1952).
4. Eugene Lowry, *The Homiletical Plot* (Atlanta: John Knox Press, 1980). See chapter 1, pp. 7-22.
5. Lynn Harold DeWolf, *Responsible Freedom: Guidelines to Christian Action* (New York: Harpers, 1971).
6. Willi Apel, *Harvard Dictionary of Music: Second Edition Revised and Enlarged* (Cambridge: Belknap Press of Harvard University, 1969), pp. 440-41.
7. In O. Richard Bowyer, Betty L. Hart, and Charlotte A. Meade, *Prayer in the Black Tradition* (Nashville: The Upper Room, 1986), p. 28.
8. Burke O. Long, *I Kings with an Introduction to Historical Literature,* ed. Rolf Knierim and Gene M. Tucker, *The Forms of the Old Testament Literature,* vol. 9 (Grand Rapids: Wm. B. Eerdmans Publishing Co., 1984), pp. 26-27.

Chapter 6: Finding the Bridges Between Our Voice
and the Community's

1. Hans W. Frei, *The Eclipse of Biblical Narrative* (New Haven: Yale University Press, 1974).
2. Michael Goldberg, *Theology and Narrative: A Critical Introduction* (Nashville: Abingdon Press, 1981).
3. Bruce Rosenberg, *The Art of the American Folk Preacher* (New York: Oxford University Press, 1970).
4. James Weldon Johnson, *God's Trombones* (New York: Viking Press, 1927).
5. Paul Laurence Dunbar, *Lyrics of Lovely Life* (New York: Dodd, Mead and Co., 1901), pp. 26-30. In a sermon in verse, entitled "An Ante-bellum Sermon," typical dialect lines are "We is gathered hyeah, my brothahs, in dis howlin' wildaness, fu' to speak some words of confo't to each othas in distress. An' we chooses fu' ouah subjic' dis—we'll splain it by an' by"; "An' de Lawd said, 'Moses, Moses,' an' de man said 'Hyeah am I.'"
6. Henry Mitchell, *Black Preaching* (Philadelphia: Lippincott, 1970).
7. Liston Pope, *Millhands and Preachers* (New Haven: Yale University Press, 1942).
8. Richard L. Eslinger, *A New Hearing* (Nashville: Abingdon Press, 1987).